Fifth Army at War

Right: Shermans of the
NZ 19th Armoured
Regiment make their way
through the ruins of
Cassino.
/*Alexander Turnbull Library,
Wellington*

Below: Anzio. The landing was virtually unopposed as this scene, photographed on X-Ray Beach, soon after dawn on 22 January shows./US Army

Fifth Army
at War

George Forty

Charles Scribner's Sons
NEW YORK

Printed in Great Britain
Library of Congress Catalog Card Number 79-93178
ISBN: 0-684-16615-1

**Right: Fifth and Eighth Army linkup.
Mark Clark greets Montgomery during
the latter's visit to the Salerno area.
/IWM**

**Below: One of the 19th Armoured
Regiment's Shermans supporting the
infantry attack./IWM**

Contents

Top left: An armoured car belonging to the 6th Duke of Connaught's Own Lancers of 8 Indian Division provides a map rest for these Indian officers as they plan an attack./*MOD New Delhi*

Left: US tanks roll ashore at Anzio from the open bow doors of an LST./*US Army*

Dedication

In dedicating this book to the men of the United States Fifth Army I can do no better than to echo the words of their great commander, Gen Mark W. Clark, from his book *Calculated Risk*:

' . . . The story I would like to tell, I thought then, is the story of the men who lie there.* Nothing can blur my memory of their courage and tenacity and devotion to duty, of their refusal to be awed by seemingly insurmountable odds, by the swirling dust of Salerno, by the treacherous mud of the Liri Valley, or by the stinging snows of the high Apennines. Some chapters of their story I could not hope to tell. No one could tell them who was not there day after day in the foxholes that filled with water before they were half dug, and on the rocky peaks where not even a pack mule could find a footing.

* Gen Clark was visiting the American cemetery at Anzio, during a trip he made back to Italy with his wife, in May 1949.

'But I can tell part of the story. I can tell how and why the turn of the wheel of war took the men of the Fifth Army to Italy and what was behind the orders that sent them into battle at Salerno, on the Volturno, at Cassino, and on the flat and barren little strip of Hell known as the Anzio beachhead; and I can give at least a glimpse of the bravery and sacrifices, not only of the Americans but of men of a dozen other nationalities who fought their way into the not-so-soft underbelly of the Axis. They are men who paid heavily for their page in history . . . I am proud to have had an opportunity to share their calculated risk in the Mediterranean.'

Below: The standards of the Fifth Army, photographed at a Thanksgiving Service held at HQ Fifth Army on 9 May 1945. */US Army*

Foreword
General Mark W. Clark
US Army, Retired

This is a story of the gallant men of the Fifth United States Army whose record made one of the most vivid chapters in the history of World War II. Through the mud and mountains of Italy these hundreds of thousands of Americans fought side by side with men of many other nationalities against the tenacious German enemy. Never was a Commander prouder of the accomplishments of his soldiers than was I. And I am particularly happy that George Forty, a Britisher whose comrades were so important a part of this army, has elected to write this combat history.

As a young officer I was a student of Napoleon's campaigns. During the difficult times in Italy I remembered one of the statements attributed to him: 'Do not be an ally, fight them.' There were men of approximately 16 nations attached to my Fifth Army, among them Americans, British, Canadians, New Zealanders, Australians, Poles, Brazilians, Frenchmen (with Tunisians, Algerians and Moroccans), South Africans, Rhodesians, Indians, Pakistanis, Greeks and Palestinians. The collection of so many different nationalities into one Army made for a complicated operation. There were different languages to be considered, different beliefs in God, a variety of equipment, ammunition and food to be supplied, and sometimes there were conflicting nationalistic ambitions. These factors combined with many others to make logistical planning inordinately difficult.

It was necessary from time to time for me to move a division held in reserve from one zone to another. Even when they were so close in heritage as the British and Americans, this operation caused problems in feeding and equipment. When the factor of language and divergent cultures was added, the problems were magnified many times. The homogeneous German forces enjoyed a very real advantage here; they could move their divisions from one front to another without logistical complications. It is to the ever-

lasting credit of my men from so many countries that through their determination they welded themselves into a United States Army and made it one of the finest fighting organizations in World War II.

I predict that this book will be of deep interest to the hundreds of thousands of men of many nationalities who passed through the ranks of the Fifth Army, and to their loved ones.

Mark W. Clark

Introduction

Of all the field armies of the United States of America, Gen Mark Clark's Fifth Army holds the record for the longest continuous period in action against the enemy in World War II, and also of course, for being the first American troops to land on Hitler's 'Festung Europa'. Not that Fifth Army was an all American force, indeed it was quite the opposite. Fifth Army was probably the most truly international of all the Allied Armies. For much of the time the strength of American troops was equalled or exceeded by a mixture of British, New Zealand, Indian, Canadian, South African, French, Brazilian and Italian contingents. It is to their great credit that such a mix of nationalities was able to function so efficiently and, for the most part, with such good sense and friendliness. In this they had the shining example of their first commander, Gen Mark W. Clark and his successor Gen Lucian K. Truscott.

As we shall see, the Fifth Army came into being in North Africa in early 1943, first went into action at Salerno in the September of that year, and from then on was never really out of action until the war was won in Italy. As well as having to face a brave, determined, well equipped and skilful enemy, who was the master of the slow withdrawal, Fifth Army and their comrades in arms, Eighth Army, had two other major handicaps. The first of these were the conditions under which they had to fight, namely the appalling terrain and weather. For much of the time they fought in rocky, inhospitable mountains, through the severe conditions of snow and ice of two dreadful winters. Not that the mud and rain, or the heat and dust of the other seasons of the year were much better in reality. Certainly, the gallant soldiers of Fifth Army had to face battle conditions probably worse than any in Europe and as bad as any in the more remote parts of the world. As one soldier wrote: 'These things . . . constitute war and battle: rain and mud, cold and discomfort . . . of digging and of sleepless nights and tiring days, of being afraid and of being hungry, of repairing roads and of building bridges, of being lonely . . . of an endless number of little things.'*

* *The Winter Line;* Historical Division of the US War Department.

They also had to face the morale sapping experience of becoming a 'Forgotten Army'. Initially, of course, they received their fair share of publicity, reinforcements, supplies etc, but predictably, once the D-Day landings 'stole the headlines', the troops in Italy suffered accordingly. This inevitably angered the soldiers and their feelings were well expressed in forces newspapers like *Stars and Stripes*, or in such bitter parodies as the refrain sung to the tune of *Lilli Marlene* which began: '*We're the D-Day Dodgers, out in Italy – always on the vino, always on the spree*', the reference to 'dodging D-Day' having supposedly been made by some stupid, unthinking British woman politician. And of course their commanders had to put up with the annoyance of having to sit by helplessly and watch a large proportion of their best troops being taken away for the 'Anvil' landings in southern France. It is easy now to

Left: Men of the Grenadier Guards move up to frontline positions-a long and steep climb. /IWM

Below: General Sir Harold Alexander, GOC of the Allied Armies in Italy, shakes hands with Gen Mark Clark after presenting him with the insignia of a Knight Commander of the Most Excellent Order of the British Empire, 29 April 1944./IWM

see with hindsight, what a difference to the current balance of power between West and East that might have been made in Europe, had Fifteenth Army Group been able to retain sufficient strength to be first into the Balkans – no wonder Stalin favoured 'Anvil', undoutedly realising that it was the perfect way of hamstringing the Allied efforts in Italy.

For the record a total of nearly 189,000 casualties were sustained by Fifth Army during the Italian campaign, of which 31,886 paid the supreme sacrifice. The breakdown was:

American – 19,475 killed; 109,642 total casualties
British and Commonwealth – 6,605 killed; 47,452 total
French – 5,241 killed; 27,671 total
Brazilian – 275 killed; 2,411 total
Italian – 290 killed; 1,570 total

What an international gathering Fifth Army was, to be sure! And in these days as memories of the war fade, it does us in Britain no harm at all to remember occasionally the brave men of the Commonwealth, of South Africa, Rhodesia, India, New Zealand, Canada, Australia and all the rest, who put their lives on the line in the defence of Great Britain, without a second thought. What a pity so many of our politicians and public figures have such conveniently short memories. Out of respect for the memory of all these gallant men, and for all the other brave members of all units of the Fifth Army, this book is written with the greatest admiration for every single one of them. I have found that all too often those who look back at such campaigns, where the Allied forces were so mixed, tend to highlight the things that went wrong, the bad points and the disagreements, rather than the far greater number of things that went right! Thank God that there were such fine fighting formations as the Fifth Army on our side, I hope this book will do just a little to keep their fine spirit alive – we could all do with some of it today.

As with all my other books in the 'At War' series I have found it an impossible task to include the full story of every battle in which 5th Army took part. What I have tried to do instead is to highlight a particular engagement in each phase of the campaign, involving one or other of the many nationalities which made up this international force. Inevitably I have missed out more acts of bravery than I have been able to include, however, I do hope that the mixture which I have put in does give at least some indication of what it was like to be a 'D-Day Dodger'.

Acknowledgements

I would like to thank everyone who has given me help and encouragement in the preparation of this book. The following list of acknowledgements is, I hope, resonably complete, however, if I have left anyone out I do hope they will forgive me!

Establishments
Historical Publications Branch, Dept of New Zealand Internal Affairs, Wellington; US Army Audio-Visual Center, Washington; Imperial War Museum, London; MOD (UK) Library, London; RUSI Library, London; Citadel Museum, South Carolina; Regt Association (UK) 9th Gurkha Rifles; Association of the United States Army; US Army Military History Institute; RHQ, The Queen's Royal Regiment; Gale & Polden Ltd; Herbert S. Benjamin Associates Inc; Establissement Cinématographique des Armées, Fort D'Ivry; National Association, 10th Mountain Division Inc; South African National Museum of Military History, Saxonwald; Regimental Museum The Green Howards; RHQ, The Duke of Wellington's Regiment; Armed Forces Film & Photo Division, MOD New Delhi; Chief of Military History and Center of Military History, US Department of the Army; 88th Infantry Division Association Inc; Services Attache, British Embassy, Rome; Ufficio Storico Dello Stato Maggiore Dell'Escercito, Rome; The Alexander Turnbull Library, Wellington; Bundersarchiv, Koblenz; Service Historique Etat Major de l'Armée de Terre; Public Information Division, Dept of US Army; Headquarter Board, The Durban Light Infantry.

Individuals
May I start by thanking Gen Mark W. Clark for his constant help and encouragement and for writing the excellent Foreword to this book. I would also like to thank: Col Robert D. Burhans, US Army Retd; Professor George F. Earle; Gen Alfred M. Gruenther, US Army Retd; Maj-Gen D. E. Isles, CB, OBE, Retd; Capt L. R. Kerr, Brazilian Embassy; Maj-Gen F. A. H. Ling, CB, CBE, DSO, DL Retd; J. S. Lucas, Esq; Bill Mauldin, Esq; Jack E. Miles, Esq; Col Neil D. Orpen, JCD; Maj-Gen Glenn K. Otis, CG 1st US Armored Division; Lt-Col P. M. Salusbury-Trelawny, MC, Retd; Col Oran C. Stovall, US Army Retd; Robert L. Wagner, Esq.

Bradford, West Yorkshire *George Forty*
March 1979

Origins and Composition

Origins

The United States Fifth Army was activated at Oudjda, French Morocco, at one minute past midnight on 5 January 1943. Its basic organisation was initially: 1st Armored Corps, located in French Morocco; II Corps, in Western Algeria, and XII Air Support Command. Its first Commanding General was Lieutenant-General Mark Wayne Clark, who had previously been Deputy C-in-C, Allied Forces in North Africa. He was to remain as CG until 16 December 1944, when he took command of 15th Army Group from Gen Sir Harold Alexander, his place in Fifth Army being taken by Gen Lucian K. Truscott, who commanded for the rest of the hostilities in Italy. The shoulder insignia was truly representative of their Moroccan origins, featuring a Moorish minaret. The insignia was designed by Col Maurice R. Barker, and officially adopted after a contest in which many other designs were received. Its colours were red, white and blue. The background was red, the minaret blue and the large letter 'A' and figure '5' were in white, an excellent choice of colours for such a truly international force, appearing as they do, on the flags of the USA, Great Britain and France.

Fifth Army's initial territorial responsibility was the area of French Morocco and Algeria west of a line running north-south through Orleansville. Their initial mission was to prepare a striking force for amphibious operations, at the same time ensuring the integrity of their territorial area in cooperation with French civil and military authorities. The striking force was to consist of not less than one armoured division and one infantry division, both fully trained in amphibious operations. Accordingly, eight training centres were established, the most important being the Invasion Training Centre at Port aux Poules, Algeria. Here training consisted of unit and individual instruction of the infantry and armoured combat teams, plus combined operations with the US Navy, the Army Air Force and the 1st Engineer Amphibian Brigade. The centre aimed at developing aggressive, fast-moving, hard hitting, sustained action. Other centres dealt with such subjects as leadership and battle training, air observation, airborne operations, tank destroyers, engineers and the training of the new French divisions being raised in North Africa, so that they would be fully conversant with the handling of the new American equipment.

Whilst this training was taking place, the staff were considering various projects for the invasion of Europe. Fifth Army was eventually detailed in late July with the task of developing plans to seize Naples and nearby airfields, 'with a view to preparing a firm base for further offensive operations.' The codename for this operation, scheduled to take place in early September 1943, was 'Avalanche'. Interwoven with the Allied plans for the invasion of Italy, were the secret negotiations with the new Italian Government under

Below: Fifth Army shoulder flash. This picture, showing Gen Mark Clark attending a midnight mass in a tiny cathedral near Naples, Christmas Eve 1943, gives an excellent view of the Fifth Army insignia. Gen Clark is accompanied by Lt-Col Art Sutherland (left) and Maj-Gen Alfred Gruenther (right)./*IWM*

Marshal Badoglio, for an armistice. The surrender document was in fact signed by the Italians on 3 September 1943, the same day as Gen Montgomery's British Eighth Army landed unopposed on the toe of Italy, having crossed the narrow Straits of Messina from Sicily. However, it had been decided to keep the surrender secret until 'Avalanche' had taken place, and Gen Dwight D. Eisenhower, C-in-C Allied Forces in the Mediterranean, didn't broadcast the announcement that hostilities had ended, until 1830 hours on 8 September 1943, when Fifth Army was steaming on its way to the Salerno beaches. The effects of this announcement were undoubtedly to relax the assaulting forces, to make them feel complacent and that their assault would be unopposed – 'a piece of cake'. They were, alas, to be jolted out of this false sense of security in the most unpleasant way the following morning.

Composition

Anyone who still has any doubts about the cosmopolitan makeup of Fifth Army should study the photographs which accompany this short section of the book. Even the American formations contained not only white and black troops, but also the renowned Nisei battalions of Japanese Americans. Composed mainly of Hawaiians of Japanese descent, the 100th Infantry Battalion, for example, was activated in June 1942 and joined the Fifth Army at Salerno on 22 September 1943. Apart from several months in southern France, they fought throughout the Italian campaign, winning a Presidential Unit Citation for the destruction of a German SS battalion on Monte Belvedere, north of Piombino, in June 1944. The battalion earned 14 Distinguished Service Crosses and 75 Silver Stars, and Gen Mark Clark makes special mention of their courage in his book *Calculated Risk*. He also mentions the problems which faced the 92nd Infantry Division, which was composed entirely of Negro soldiers. However, he does make the point, conveniently forgotton by many of their critics, that he personally decorated many Negro officers and men of the division for bravery, and that many others were killed performing extremely brave acts on the battlefield. New Zealanders, Indians and South African soldiers reflect the strength of the Commonwealth representation in the British contingent and the epic stories of their bravery are well known, but often forgotten.

Right: American GIs. Eleven US divisions served with Fifth Army. These GIs were photographed in the Piazzi di la Republica, Bologna on 21 April 1945.
/*US Army*

12

Right: British Tommies. There were seven British divisions which served with 5th Army in Italy. These Tommies were bivouacking in an old Roman amphitheatre on the Garigliano front, March 1944./IWM

It is also interesting to see members of the 25,000 strong Brazilian Expeditionary Forces who arrived in Italy in August 1944. Their first action on 15 September was the capture of the village of Massarora, north of Lake Massaciuccoli and they were the first South American soldiers *ever* to fight on European soil.

Perhaps a list of the main formations that were at one time or another part of Fifth Army would be useful here:

American
1st Armored Division
3rd Infantry Division
10th Mountain Division
34th Infantry Division
36th Infantry Division
45th Infantry Division
82nd Airborne Division
85th Infantry Division
88th Infantry Division
91st Infantry Division
92nd Infantry Division

British and Commonwealth
1st British Infantry Division
2nd New Zealand Infantry Division
4th Indian Infantry Division
5th British Infantry Division
6th British Armoured Division
6th South African Armoured Division
7th British Armoured Division
8th Indian Infantry Division
46th British Infantry Division
56th British (London) Infantry Division
78th British Infantry Division
other troops included 1st Canadian Armoured Brigade

French
1st Motorised Infantry Division
2nd Moroccan Infantry Division
3rd Algerian Infantry Division
4th Moroccan Mountain Division
other troops included the 1st, 3rd and 4th Groups of Tabors

Brazilian
1st Infantry Division

Italian
1st Italian Motorised Group
Legano Combat Group

Above: Indian soldiers man
a PIAT. Men of the 1/5
Mahratta Light Infantry of
8 Indian Infantry Division
who, with 4 Indian
Infantry Division, served
with Fifth Army. The
Projector Infantry Anti-
Tank fired a hollow
charge grenade about
100yd./MOD New Delhi

Above right: Springboks of
6 SA Division. Gen Smuts,
South African Prime
Minister, talks to a group
of Springbok sappers.
/SA National Museum of
Military History

Right: French Guard of
Honour. Gen Mark Clark
inspects a French guard
accompanied by Gen
Alphonse Juin (left) at the
headquarters of the French
Expeditionary Corps./IWM

Below right: Brazilian
troops arrive. Smiling
Brazilian troops arrive in
Naples on 16 July 1944.
/IWM

Left: Kiwi AA gunners.
Men of the 2nd New
Zealand Division man their
40mm Bofors AA gun on
the alert for enemy planes
near Cassino, 15 March
1944.
/Alexander Turnbull Library,
Wellington

Above: Japanese Americans
engage snipers. Men of the
famous Nisei battalions
man their mortar – the
standard US light infantry
mortar./*IWM*

Right: A Negro patrol in
action. Men of the all
Negro 92nd Infantry
Division engage an enemy
machine gun nest near
Lucca./*IWM*

Below right: Italian
soldiers fight for the Allies.
A Fifth Army GI inspects
a 'Moschetto automatico
modello 38A'
manufactured by Beretta
and one of their most
widely used weapons.
/*IWM*

Salerno

The First Hours

'At 2350 the flagship *Samuel Chase* stopped her engines and lay about 10 miles from the beaches south of the Sele River. The transports formed in three lines, followed by three more lines of landing ships and landing craft. The moon set at 0057, making concealment easier but increasing the difficulties of navigation to the shore. The sea was smooth, the wind north to north-east, and the sky almost clear. An armada of 450 vessels lay ready for H-Hour. Some 50 more vessels of all types were prepared for the first follow-up. The Fifth Army of 100,000 British troops and 69,000 American troops with some 20,000 vehicles, was poised for a major attack over the Salerno beaches.'

That is how the US Army's Historical Division described the scene in the Bay of Salerno, just before H-Hour. The 15 miles of beaches, every yard of which would be used for landing some part of the invasion force, lay in an enormous arc, stretching from Salerno to Paestum. On the morning of 9 September 1943 mist covered the mountains to the north and east, but later this would clear to give the Germans an uninterrupted view of the entire beachhead area.

'The plain at the foot of the mountains was quite flat as far as the main coastal road, beyond which the ground began to swell violently into the lower foothills. Almost the entire area of the plain was under intensive cultivation and was speckled with farms. The

Below: Map 1 The Salerno Landings, 9 September 1943.

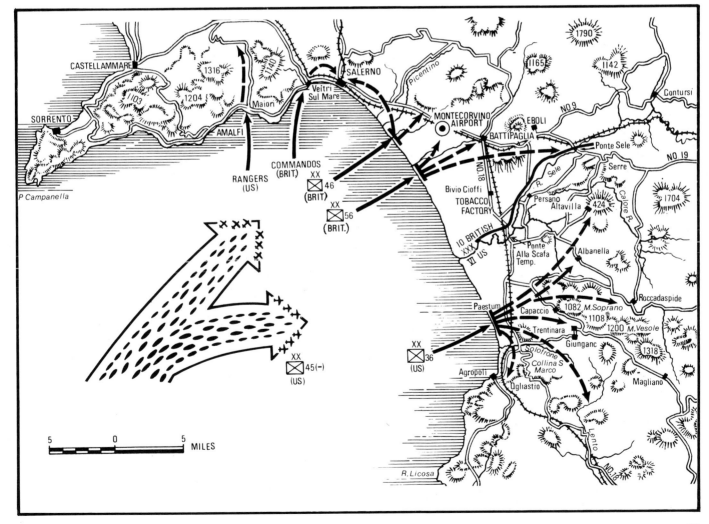

wheat had just been cut, but the tobacco plants and vines still stood eight feet high in the fields. The ground was intersected by a network of dykes and ditches, some filled with water and some concreted, and the river meandered across the plain in wide, flat beds, forming in places marshes and deep pools. The military import of these natural features was threefold. In the first place, it was not easy for infantry to see their way ahead nor to move silently in deployed formation through the high, thick crops. In the second place, the ditches made it impossible for lorries and carriers, and difficult for tanks to move across the open country: they were confined to the few roads and narrow tracks, where one breakdown or one unlucky shell-burst would block the progress of the remainder of the column behind. And, in the third place, the supreme importance of seizing the mountain crests became even more evident than the study of maps and air photos had suggested many weeks before.'*

The opening days of September 1943 had seen the Allies begin their determined assault on the mainland of Europe, with Gen Montgomery's Eighth Army striking the first blow with their 'Baytown' operation across the Straits of Messina from Sicily, to land on the Calabrian coast on 3 September. Whilst this landing was taking place, the convoys for 'Avalanche', Fifth Army's Salerno landings, and 'Slapstick', Eighth Army's second landing – this time in the Gulf of Taranto – left North Africa. In brief terms, the 'Avalanche' landings were aimed at capturing the hills which surrounded the coastal plain, and, once sufficient troops were ashore, to push northwards through the hills to capture Naples. As the map shows, the attack was two pronged, with the British 10th Corps in the north and the American VI Corps in the south. Units from the 46th and 56th Divisions would form the assault waves of 10 Corps, whilst 36th Division would land in the VI Corps beachhead area, with 45th Division close behind as follow-up force. An integral part of the plan were landings by US Rangers and British Commandos north of 10 Corps beaches, with the tasks of capturing the vital passes through the mountains, which guarded the shortest route to Naples. Three Ranger battalions were to capture and hold the Nocera defile, while two British commando units were assigned similar missions for the La Molina defile. In addition, the commandos were given a secondary task of destroying a coast-defence battery which commanded the western part of the Bay of Salerno.

* *The Grenadier Guards 1939-45;* Capt Nigel Nicolson and Patrick Forbes.

18

Above left: Loading up the LSTs for 'Avalanche'. An armoured command vehicle, belonging to 7th Armoured Division is loaded through the bow doors of a landing ship. This famous British Division was the floating reserve for 10 Corps. /A. Potter

Centre left: Salerno, soon after the landings. /A. Potter

Bottom left: Scene on one of the 10 Corps beaches as landing operations go forward./IWM

Above: British AA gunners man a Bofors 40mm LAA gun as landing operations continue. In the centre of the photo is a good shot of the DUKW (Truck, amphibious 2½ ton, 6 x 6) which was used so successfully during many amphibious landings. It was 36ft long and 8ft wide, over 21,000 were built during World War II and continued to give excellent service for many years after the war./IWM

Right: Pfc Charles E. 'Commando' Kelly of 36 Infantry Division was the first soldier to earn the Congressional Medal of Honor awarded to US ground forces in Europe during World War II, for his heroism at the Salerno landings./US Army

Above: German troops in action during the Allied landings./*IWM*

As the eye-witness accounts that follow explain, the announcement of the Italian surrender which was broadcast to the invasion forces as they neared the Italian coast, did much to take away their 'edge' and to lull many into a false sense of security. They would unfortunately discover the hard way that the beach defences were ready for them and that Gen Kesselring's forces would fiercely contest the landings. A bitter and hardfought battle lay ahead as they carried out their last minute preparations for disembarking. I have chosen four accounts of the landings and the initial battles which followed, one from each of the four divisions mentioned above. Starting in the north, here is an extract from a privately published history: *The Story of 46 Division 1939-1945*:

'It was no calm blue Mediterranen sea the first day out, and the respite from sea-sickness which a call in Sicily afforded was more than welcome. In bays that had been cleared of their inhabitants our troops were fed and accomodated by the American Army. Early next morning the convoy got under way again, and during the day was joined by innumerable others, so that as far as the eye could see there were ships of all sizes moving inevitably towards Italy. The four assaulting divisions were on the seas. In the afternoon a lone German recce plane flew low and fast over the invasion fleet. Later bombers appeared, and intermittent attacks continued through the growing darkness. One LCT was hit, and the glow lit up the night sky, already

streaked with lines of tracer which pointed at the attacking aircraft. At dusk, over the ships' speakers came the startling BBC announcement of Italy's unconditional surrender, which seemed to accord strangely with the falling bombs. But it was midnight before Gen Hawkesworth received official notification of the surrender, which added that covering fire on the beaches was to proceed as planned,* but that the coastal batteries were only to be engaged if they opened fire (these were presumed to manned by Italians). Shortly afterwards coastal guns did open fire, and were engaged by the *Mendip*, *Brecon* and *Blakeney*. Hopes of easy success began to wane.

'With the crash of guns overhead the assault boats began to move shorewards in steady lines. The first wave was exactly to time. In the faint moonlight it was impossible to distinguish any of the landmarks that had been studied on the aerial photographs. The rocket ships opened up for the final five minutes battering of Red and Green beaches. 88s were joining in the incredible uproar. For the men of 46th Division it was the central moment of the war. Behind lay North Africa's early losses and eventual sudden victory; ahead were unknown battles in a new country. As inevitably as Time itself the assault boats moved forward in their appointed order to the Salerno beaches. Crouched in a crowded, living darkness men were aware more than at any other time of the relentless compulsion of the military machine, which had collected and moulded them and at a fixed hour set them down on the shores of Europe. The rocket ship opposite Green beach unloaded its barrage half a mile south of Magazzino, and the boats on the right, following up, landed 2 Hampshires on the wrong side of the Asa river. The beach was raked by machine gun fire from unblasted posts around the Magazzino, and shells tore up the sand. The first wave of men dashed forward across the open beach and by the time 5 Hampshires landed 50 minutes later only one machine gun was firing out on the right. A mile away on Red beach there was only light opposition, but S mines caused 1/4 Hampshires delay and casualties. With clockwork regularity the succeeding waves of landing craft were coming in, and men and early vehicles began to pile up on the two beaches until there was room to move forward. Further north, beyond Salerno, both the Commandos and the Rangers reported successful landings.

'Dawn came with a mist over the broad bay and the thick smoke of many deliberate screens. Landing craft churned back and

* This was only on the 10th Corps beaches, 36 Division would land without any preliminary bombardment of any kind.

Above: Going ashore at the double. GIs landing to reinforce the beachhead. Note the M2 water cooled version of the Browning .50 machine gun, used for AA defence on the back of the truck./*US Army*

forward, aircraft droned above, and the great warships of the fleet, standing offshore, added their crashing salvoes to the busy confusion. On shore the situation was obscure. On the left, from their landing on Red beach, 1/4 Hampshires had made good progress through the thick vines and low trees in face of sniping and the occasional surprise appearance of a German halftrack. They crossed the main road and occupied their final positions on the low hills beyond. On the right two of their companies were involved in confused and isolated fighting. 160 prisoners were taken, mainly Italian artillerymen. From Green beach, on the other hand, little direct headway had been made. Early in the morning a demand from the beachmaster brought companies of the KOYLI and the Lincolns ashore. But the sun was up and from the hills the enemy had obsevation over the beach. Accurate shelling scored hits on discharging LSTs, and as no suitable assembly area for vehicles had yet been gained, it was decided to suspend the disembarkation on Green beach, which already had all the appearance of a battleground with blazing jeeps and here and there a stranded, burning LST.

'Ahead, the main body of 2 and 5 Hampshires had crossed the Asa, and were half a mile inland, with 5 Hampshires on the right more or less in their planned forming-up place (they were reserve battalion). Touch had been lost with one company which had been detached to deal with opposition on the right, and had advanced inland without crossing the

Asa. This company, with little resistance, reached the airfield south of Pontecagnano. On the other flank a company of 2 Hampshires advanced to Pontecagnano itself, where their appearance surprised several German officers driving down the road in their staff cars and where their continued presence acted as a threat to the rear of the counter-attack which later developed on Green beach. The KOYLI and the Lincolns were preparing to advance when the counter-attack started. They quickly positioned themselves among the dunes within a few hundred yards of the sea. Tanks came down the narrow stone-walled track – Hampshire Lane – and the Hampshires were driven back to Magazzino, where the two headquarters took up their position with about 50 men. The remainder had not all by any means been overrun, but contact had been lost with them; small groups held out here and there and later rejoined their battalions, when the confusion of the first day's fighting was over. Indeed the battle had developed into a series of isolated, independent actions of which headquarters could not pretend to have any control, or even much knowledge. The KOYLI, for instance, were fighting without their headquarters which had landed with one company on Red beach.

'While Green beach was the scene of these disjointed battles, and had in fact almost been driven in, disembarkation was proceeding normally on Red beach. There was only one exit from the beach, a narrow road with dykes either side where several of the earlier flights of vehicles were ditched. At this point there was a long patient line of congested traffic. At one o'clock, in order to clarify the position, Gen Hawkesworth put all the troops on the right under command 128 Brigade (this had in effect already taken place, in face of the enemy's counter-attack). Brig James found himself with the remnants of two Hampshire battalions, and companies of the KOYLI, the Lincolns and later the Leicesters, holding a narrow stretch of dunes covering Green beach, and ahead a fluid situation with active enemy tanks and self-propelled guns. During the afternoon there was little change, until in the early evening the enemy began to withdraw, and the complicated process of sorting out commenced.

'At the same time Gen Hawkesworth ordered 138 Brigade HQ to land and take over command of the left sector, where considerable headway had been made and where supporting arms were piling up on Red beach. The situation which greeted Brig Harding when he landed an hour later was as follows: the Commandos and Rangers were holding fast at Vietri and Maori north of Salerno; 1/4 Hampshires were in position on the low hills across the Salerno road. On and beyond Red beach were the York and Lancasters less one company and without transport. B Squadron 46 Recce Regiment, which had landed with a limited scale of vehicles, nearly two troops of 71 Field Regiment, part of 232 Anti-Tank Battery and part of 271 Field Company. Having gleaned this information Brig Harding ordered B Squadron, with the Sappers, to move up the Salerno road and make contact with the Commandos, drop the Sappers to clear the port, and push on through the Vietri defile. Meanwhile the newly formed brigade group was concentrating and in the late afternoon the York and Lancs were ordered to advance and take the high ground east of Salerno and block the Sanseverino road.

'B Squadron moved off at half past four. The main street of Salerno was blocked by demolitions but a detour was easily found through the side streets. Few civilians were about. At the western end of the town contact was made with 2 Commando, who had had a hard day's fighting, and were glad of this first junction with 46 Division. The Squadron pushed on up the winding road through the Vietri defile and entered Cava. A German soldier was picked up wandering about the streets and he gave information of the first importance: 25 tanks and 500 infantry were harboured in the valley a mile and a half beyond the town. As dusk was falling, it was decided to withdraw to Vietri. Before leaving Cava the Squadron was feted by a great crowd of civilians in the main square, and one officer was asked by the mayor to make a speech. But

it was a fortnight before British troops were again in Cava, and by that time the town was in ruins. The York and Lancs in the evening also moved forward into Salerno and took up positions some miles east of the town on the high ground overlooking the Sanseverino road.

'On Green beach, too, the situation had improved with the gradual withdrawal of enemy tanks. The Lincolns and the KOYLI probed forward up the tracks from the beach towards Pontegagnano, which a KOYLI company reached in time to ambush and capture a small enemy road convoy. In the evening 139 Brigade landed and moved forward to their planned concentration area, which was still outside the firm perimeter of the beachhead. It was found that the wood which was to harbour their vehicles was quite impenetrable, and they came back to spend an uncomfortable night nearer the beach. So, by the evening of D-Day, the main body was ashore and the unloading was going ahead. Out of the confusion which the enemy's unexpected strength and determination had brought about, a beginning was being made to reorganise the brigades into cohesive groups. Opposition had temporarily slackened.'

The 'Black Cats' Come Ashore

On the beaches below 46 Division, the men of the 56th (London) Infantry Division, who wore the emblem of Dick Whittington's famous cat as their divisional sign, had also started to land. Here is how their privately published history – entitled *The Black Cats at War* recalled the landing:

'The night of 8/9 September was fine; there was a bright moon and the sea was calm. The convoy anchored some nine miles from the Italian shore and then begun the task of transferring the assault troops of the first wave into smaller craft. They had already donned their coffee-dipped khaki drill (it was too warm for battle-dress and the colour of the khaki drill too light to afford protection once on the mainland, hence the liberal use of coffee); the small landing craft chugged their way towards the beaches, encountering a heavy swell as they neared land. The moon waned and the first streaks of dawn threw into prominent relief the mountains of the Appenine range. All was quiet. The forward elements of 167 Brigade had been first away and at 0350 hours, 8 Royal Fusiliers and 7 Oxford and Bucks Light Infantry leapt into the shallow water and scrambled onto the beach. They were quickly followed by the 9th Royal Fusiliers. Fortunately for them the current had carried them slightly off course and they had overshot the point at which they were meant to land and on which the Germans had anticipated a landing. They had mined it very thoroughly and 167 Brigade would undoubtedly have suffered many casualties but for the vagaries of the tide. Suddenly all hell was let loose. The German coastal batteries opened up and an ammunition ship was hit. The guns of the warships thundered in reply and the Luftwaffe made a sortie. And still the troops poured ashore. The beach soon presented a picture of organised chaos. There were Bren carriers darting about, then the guns and the heavier transport came ashore and as quickly as they could made their way to the de-water-proofing points. Not all got there and it was immaterial whether they were deproofed or not. Soon after 9 o'clock the 8 RF reported tanks threatening their right flank and shortly afterwards four of their portees, together with some ammunition were hit and destroyed. The German high velocity batteries inland were making the beaches extremely uncomfortable. These were eventually rendered ineffective by the Navy's guns, but not before they had done a lot of damage and caused many casualties. The pumping station which normally reg-ulated the draining of the fertile plain beyond the beaches was out of action, with the result that the flow of water in the canal and dykes was rapid and in places overflowed the banks. The fields immediately off the beaches became waterlogged, making the progress of the tanks and tracked vehicles almost impossible. In-deed, elements of the Royal Scots Greys in support of the Fusiliers were soon in trouble, at least eight of their tanks being "bellied". Around noon three enemy tanks emerged from among some buildings ahead of 167 Brigade HQ and advanced along the road. Anti-tank guns were rushed up and eventually a troop of the Greys knocked out the tanks.'

The 'T' Patchers Land

The southern arm of the two pronged landings was led by the 36th US Infantry Division – 'The Texas Army' who proudly wore as their divisional shoulder patch a grey Indian arrowhead emblazoned with a green capital 'T' in its centre. Among their number was Andrew F. Price, a vintage lieutenant-colonel with the 141st Infantry Regiment. He had fought in World War I as an under-age volunteer and was now a member of the first American divison to set foot on the continent of Europe in World War II. He wrote after-wards:

'We were five days crossing the blue Medi-terranean heavily convoyed. The day before we were to land the news was flashed that Italy had surrendered her Army and Navy. We had the battleships *Boise* and *Savannah* and a number of cruisers with us.* They were

to give us naval preparation fire. This was called off because they did not want to kill civilians or to destroy the property of our new friends the Italians. This has never been done since Salerno, all amphibious operations are preceded by strong naval fire . . . At 2am on the morning of 9 September we went over the side of the ship, using landing nets. We were nine miles off the coast and we were due to hit the beach at 3.30am – 141st Infantry on the right and 142nd Infantry on the left and 143rd in reserve. It was quite a thrill to go over the side of a ship on landing nets, loaded down with combat equipment. It was 45ft straight down, in the dark. I sure was glad when my feet hit that boat. The assault boat had a 36 passenger capacity. Mine had 20 men and my regimental radio jeep. Nine miles of sea in such a craft is a long way too.'

It had been hoped for a surprise landing in the 36 Division area, hence the absence of any preparatory barrage. However, all hope of this succeeding was quickly shattered when a strident metallic sounding voice boomed out over a loudspeaker, in English, to the troops approaching the beaches in their frail craft: 'Come on in and give up. We have got you covered.'†

Col Price's narrative continues:
'The Germans were expecting us and the beach was heavily defended by crack German troops . . . The beaches were alive with tracer fire from machine guns and rifle fire. Barbed wire, booby traps, trip wires, concrete and steel emplacements, underwater ob-stacles and artillery positions everywhere. All this and no artillery or naval fire to precede our landing. It was just plain unadulterated hell, crossing those beaches. At dawn the Huns sent tanks against us, we had nothing to fight them with except that which we carried in our hands, the bazookas. They were kept buttoned up tight with accurate rifle fire and many were destroyed by the bazookas. But it was like fighting tanks bare handed. At 9.30am one piece of artillery was landed, a 105mm from Battery C, 131st Field Artillery. It was fired at everything as fast as it could be fired and it sure was a welcome piece. I saw riflemen swarm over the top of moving German tanks trying to shoot through slits or throw grenades inside. Other tanks would machine gun them off. They ran over wounded men and officers and spun their treads. At 12.30 permission was finally given for the Navy to open up. Those big guns sure sounded good. Soon it

---

* Actually Col Price's ship recognition was not strictly accurate, as the *Boise*, *Savannah* and *Philadelphia* which protected the convoy together with a covey of destroyers, were in fact cruisers.

† There seems to be some doubt as to whether this actually happened. The story appears in the US Historical Division's book about the landing and in many other accounts of the landings, however, Gen Fred Walker, CG 36 Division, denied that it ever did happen, or that any of his units mentioned it in their reports.

Above: British troops enter Salerno town past rows of anti-tank obstacles./IWM

Right: British infantry passing two knocked out enemy tanks on the main road near Pasanara./IWM

Below right: Carrying infantry on their backs, Shermans of 40th RTR pass a road block as they leave Salerno town en route for Naples, 15 September 1944. /IWM

was possible to land the cannon company, anti-tank company and more artillery. This was followed by our tanks. It was some days before a secure beachhead had been established and it required uncommon courage and endurance to wrestle this beach away from the pride of the German army. The cost – one out of three were casualties in my division at Salerno.'

Acts of Bravery

On all the beaches there were many acts of bravery as American and British soldiers fought doggedly to maintain their foothold on the enemy coastline. Here are but a few of the many incidents which Robert L. Wagner mentions in his book *The Texas Army*:

'Pvt J. C. Jones of Company C from Sanger, Texas, found himself on the beach with a large group of men who were walking aimlessly back and forth. He gathered about 50 together and led them toward the battalion objective. Under heavy fire they knocked out a number of enemy gun positions; Jones himself was killed in action a few days later. . . . Sgt Manuel S. Gonzales of Company F discovered the position of a German 88mm field piece whose fire was creating havoc among the landing craft. The German gun crew spotted him creeping toward them and set his back pack afire with a machine gun burst. Gonzales, from Fort Davies, Texas, calmly worked his way forward, exchanging hand grenades with the defenders. Though wounded by grenade fragments, he killed the gun crew and blew up their ammunition. . . . Lt Robert H. Carey, from Waterville, Maine, was fired upon soon after landing by three Germans armed with machine pistols. He returned their fire with his carbine – killing one. His weapon having jammed, he rushed upon his attackers, knocked one of them down with his carbine, then tackled the third, taking him prisoner . . . Beyond the beaches in front of the 141st, the relatively flat terrain was now invaded by five Mark IV (medium) tanks. The German armour rolled over the American troops who had taken cover in the irrigation ditches, firing continual machine gun bursts into the prone men as they rumbled by. A platoon of B Company, led by Staff Sgt James A. Whitaker of Brownwood, Texas, was caught by these tanks. Whitaker emptied his sub-machine gun clip into the driving aperture of one tank while machine gun fire from the vehicle stitched him across the legs. As he lay wounded on the ground he reloaded and opened fire again. The tank turned and lumbered away. Whitaker's coolness undoubtedly prevented many casualties in his platoon . . . A member of Company L, Pfc Harry J. Keefer of Harrisburg, Pennsylvania, attacked an enemy machine gun nest with his Browning Automatic Rifle,

Above: American troops in Altavilla which was not finally captured until 17 September. Liberated civilians can be seen reading a poster put up by the Allied Military Government./*US Army*

destroying it. As he did so, he was hit and killed by a second automatic weapon. When Keefer's body was recovered his lifeless finger was still pressed against the trigger. . . . The 2nd Battalion of the 141st, landing 50 minutes late, passed through rear elements of 3rd Battalion and proceeded along the 3rd's left flank towards its objective. Companies E and F pressed inland until halted by eight German tanks running back and forth across both company fronts. The tanks inflicted numerous casualties with their machine guns until they were forced to retreat by the effects of infantry weapons alone. In the fight Cpl Benito G. Dominguez of Seguin, Texas, knocked out an enemy halftrack with a rifle grenade. Pvt Raymond G. Guttierz of Senora, Texas, moved forward firing his BAR. Two enemy bullets pierced his helmet but failed to touch him. The third caught him in the arm. He continued to advance, located the enemy machine gun, closed in on it, and knifed the German gunner to death.'

Similar acts of heroism were taking place in the British area, 9 Royal Fusiliers, for example, managed to get into the vitally important village of Battipaglia, but were forced out when the enemy counter-attacked, suffering heavy casualties including their commanding officer. The second in command, Maj Delforce, took over and under his inspired leadership – he was awarded a DSO for his bravery – the 9th gave a splendid account of themselves. In fact one platoon was not driven out of the village and found itself isolated. The men managed to hide up successfully in a loft directly over a room occupied by the Germans, until the place was eventually recaptured! There were enemy tank attacks on the British beaches as well and in one such battle, 64 Field Regiment engaged the enemy over open sights, shooting up a number of tanks at very short range and putting the survivors to flight.

The RAF played its part in the battle with Mustangs and Spitfires engaging ground targets, whilst the naval guns of such vessels as HMS *Warspite* and the USS *Philadelphia* fairly blistered the roads inland, shooting up enemy transport and communications. Although glad to have the fire support some of the troops found the experience of friendly shells almost brushing their cheeks a little disconcerting. As one young Fusilier put it afterwards 'we were bloody nearly shaved by those shells!' One US admiral, Admiral Connolly earned himself the nickname 'Close-in-Connolly', when he took his flagship inshore to engage an enemy battery which he had personally spotted firing into the LCTs from a position south-east of Salerno.

The 'Thunderbirds' Join the Action

The 45th US Infantry Division were in the follow-up wave, the first landing craft of 179th Infantry arriving on the beaches in the early hours of 10 September. While the rest of the division was arriving it was decided that a combat team based upon the 2nd Battalion of the 179th, supported by B Battery of 160th Field Artillery, would seize and hold the hills in the vicinity of Serre, about five miles east of Eboli. Their march continued through the night in two columns, both encountering strong enemy groups of tanks and infantry, and, during the morning of the 11th, the Germans succeeded in cutting off part of the force. Here is how Cpl Charles F. Reynolds remembered the incident in a privately published history of 45 Division:
'I left the battery position with Lt Fourte, to go on reconnaissance. Pvt Stemm was the jeep driver, and T/5 Gilbert Wailes was radio operator. We accompanied the Battalion Commander and the rest of the recce parties to the new position areas, passing several infantry companies on the way which were moving up during the night. My party returned to the battery position after daylight. The battery, which was ready to move, pulled out a few minutes later with my party at the head of the column to guide them to their new position. We went up the same route we had used the night before. The bridge across the Sele River was still burning, but the engineers had built a crossing. The trucks moved up to a large Italian house beside the road some distance from the river and halted. An Italian civilian from the house came down to the jeep and told me in French that there were still some Germans left in the woods to

26

Above: First into Naples. The crew of the leading armoured car of A Squadron of the King's Dragoon Guards pose with welcoming civilians, 0930 hours 1 October 1943. /*IWM*

Above left: A relatively peaceful scene in a small town in the Salerno area, 18 September, as two American Tank Destroyers pause before continuing their advance. /*US Army*

Left: Generals Alexander, Mark Clark and McCreery (left to right) walk along the Salerno beach after a day spent touring the area. /*IWM*

Bottom left: Mark Clark strides through the streets of Naples shortly after its capture by his troops. /*IWM*

our left. I told Lt Fourte what the Italian said, then we led the column on up the road. A minute or two later we heard machine gun fire coming from near the river and received a radio report that the rear elements of our column were being fired upon by enemy machine guns. We continued up the road until we were ordered into position. Only three of our guns had arrived, so the battery commander sent my party back to find out what was going on and what had happened to the fourth gun section and the remainder of the battery.

'We went back to the Italian building and stopped in front of it. We were joined there by Maj Jones, Battalion S3. From there the machine gun fire sounded very near. Maj Jones, Lt Fourte and I went inside the building and looked out through a rear window but could see nothing. The three of us then went on foot down across the road to the woods. We saw several Germans. We watched for a while. Lt Fourte went back and got a .03 (1903 Springfield) rifle. We lost sight of the Germans when they moved back into the trees. I was a few yards behind Lt Fourte, behind a large steel water tank of some kind. The Germans spotted me and opened fire with rifles. The first shots missed me, but then a bullet went through the third finger of my left hand. I returned fire with my carbine and probably hit one German who was about 75yd away. Another shot got me in the upper left arm. I figured that they could keep on hitting me as long as I stayed in that position,

so I ran back to where the Lieutenant was. A bullet tore a chunk out of my right side before I hit the ground and got under cover. The Germans opened up on us with a machine pistol, besides rifles. We crawled 75-100yd through the bushes and trees and reached the road, which was out in the open. Lt Fourte ran across it first and was barely missed by rifle and machine gun fire. An enemy machine gun was firing straight up the road. I waited a few minutes and then ran across myself, but I was not fired at.

'Lt Fourte had already gone back to the jeep, thinking I was following close behind him. I went in the back door of the house, intending to go out the front way. Some Italian soldiers quartered there, seeing I was wounded, insisted that I let a doctor dress my wounds. He was attempting to do so, although he had nothing but my first aid kit, when the Lieutenant and Major came in. They had come back to look for me, thinking I had passed out. There were about 30 casualties at the aid station when I arrived. The men were talking about the enemy tanks that had broken through – saying that we were entirely surrounded by the enemy. The medics scattered some of the wounded along a dry creek bed for better protection, but the enemy tanks did not get that far.'

The battle to retain their tenuous positions went on throughout 11, 12 and 13 September, the latter being one of the hardest day's fighting that many units of the division ever experienced during the war. As darkness fell, the tanks and infantry were fighting at such close quarters that it was difficult for the tank crews to distinguish friend from foe. Typical of this fighting is a story told by Sgt Hubert M. Gilliland of Battery A, 185th Field Artillery:

'I was mess sergeant, and in view of the fact that we were eating C and K rations, the duties weren't sufficient to keep all the section busy. I turned the section over to the First Cook and assigned myself to the First Gun Section. In the late afternoon of September 13 we were informed that enemy vehicles were coming our way, approaching a bridge that the Engineers were finishing. This meant that our right flank was exposed. A truck driver and myself armed ourselves with a rocket launcher and six rounds of ammunition and went into position as a team in a bomb crater within plain sight of the bridge. Our observation plane flew low over the first field piece and the observer shouted from the window that 25 enemy tanks were approaching the bridge. I turned my rocket launcher over to another and rejoined the First Section. We started throwing shells over the trees behind the bridge, affording cover for the engineers who were withdrawing. The 189th Field

Artillery Battalion's anti-tank section were in position with their 37mm guns. We threw a withering fire into the sector around the bridge. Two shells landed within 50yd of our piece, but in the excitement they went practically unnoticed.

'By this time, the Battery's four .50 calibre guns were in position on our skirmish line. All the Engineer's personnel and equipment was now safely behind us except for one bulldozer and a quarter ton vehicle. Our .50 calibres laid down a barrage while a corporal of the 189th sauntered down to the bridge and brought the bulldozer back intact. "Tell the Engineers where this damned thing is", he said and walked away. The driver of the quarter ton saved his vehicle with equal coolness. We could hear machine gun fire and see where it was hitting. We couldn't see where it was coming from. The driver of the quarter ton said he knew where it was coming from; he had seen the location of the house and could point it out through the trees. The chief of section asked him to sight down the tube and identify the target, then we fired two rounds with delay fuses. He asked if they hit left or right of the target. "If they weren't exactly in there, they were right," the driver said. The sergeant gave "Left 10" and then we fired two more with fuse delays. In a matter of seconds something was burning beyond the line of trees. We heard small arms ammunition burning, punctuated by an occasional loud explosion. We never heard the machine gun fire again.

'I've never seen anything so perfect as the way those gun crews performed that day, or the way the 105s cut through the trees and bushes. It looked just like a giant scythe lopping them off. No living creature could have withstood such fire. I returned to the bomb crater just after Capt Miller and our first sergeant had completed the establishment of an "infantry line of defence". It was made up of every man who could be spared without affecting the efficiency of the artillery fires. They placed the line on the forward slope of the high ground overlooking the river in the direction of the line of the attack. That skirmish line turned the tide of the attack which might have cost us Salerno. Anti-tank guns were arranged just in case anything went wrong.

'I was up there all night. At about 2300 hours we were reinforced by a platoon of infantry out of the 179th. We left our .50 calibres and our gunners to reinforce the infantry. They told us our defence line was well formed by the infantry's standards. Then, for the first time in its history, Battery A of the 158th Field Artillery Battalion quietly withdrew 3,000yd to the rear. Gen McLain came along and told us to dig in and prepare for anything. He looked solemn and we decided the situation was critical. We dug in, and those were the most elaborate installations we have ever had. I'm sure we could have withstood anything the enemy could attack us with, if they had broken through.'

A Near Run Thing

In his book *Calculated Risk*, Gen Mark Clark calls the chapter in which he tells the story of the Salerno landings 'A Near Disaster', and clearly it was, as Wellington would have said, 'a damned near run thing'. However, despite the ferocity of the German attacks the men of Fifth Army managed to hang on to their beachheads, aided in no small way by the combined firepower of the Allied naval and air forces. With the Eighth Army advancing slowly but surely up from the south, the front was eventually stabilised and the Germans forced to withdraw towards their main defensive line – the Gustav Line – which ran along the Gargliano and Sangro Rivers. Monty had this to say about his Army's part in turning the tide: '. . . I have never thought we had much real influence on the Salerno problem; I reckon General Clark had got it well in hand before we arrived.' By the 16th the tide had turned sufficiently for Mark Clark to issue a congratulatory order to his men:

'As your Army Commander I want to congratulate every officer and enlisted man of the Fifth Army on the accomplishment of their mission of landing on the western coast of Italy. All the more splendid is your achievement when it is realised that it was accomplished against determined enemy resistance at the beaches. Every foot of our advance has been contested.

'We have arrived at our initial objective – our beachhead is secure. Additional troops are landing every day, and we are here to stay. Not one foot of ground will be given up.

'General Montgomery's battle-proven Eighth British Army, our partner in the task of clearing the German forces out of Italy, is advancing rapidly from the south, and in a matter of hours its presence will be felt by the enemy. Side by side with the Eighth Army, the Fifth Army will advance to occupy Naples, Rome and other cities to the north and to free Italy from German domination.

'I am highly gratified by the efficient manner wherever the British and American troops have worked side by side in mutual support, each being proud to serve by the side of the other. Their performance has justified the confidence placed in them by the people of the United Nations. They know that we shall drive on relentlessly until our job is done.'

Fifth Army's first mission had been successfully achieved.

A Toast to the Infantry

Before going any further with our story of Fifth Army's progress through Italy, I would like to include what I think are some good down to earth descriptions of the job of the infantry soldier in battle. Fifth Army was very much 'infantry orientated', principally because the difficult mountainous country in which they fought so many of their battles, was impossible going for armour. Besides, the final reckoning on the battlefield has always been a very personal affair in which the infantry soldier plays a major role. These three short descriptions all come from the fighting in Italy and the first is taken from a privately published history of the US 88th Infantry Division – 'The Blue Devils' – and I am very grateful to their Association for allowing me to quote from it. I will be telling the story of their first action later, but now a toast to the 'PBI':*

'The Air Corps "pulverises" and "obliterates" targets; the artillery "blasts" enemy installations, and the tankers "smash through" stone walls of opposition. That's the way it is always done. But despite the preparatory assaults, and the glowing adjectives, the infantryman in any battle is the deciding factor. To the infantryman falls the toughest job. When the bombers have finished their runs and the artillery has dumped its shells, the infantryman must rise out of his foxhole, charge the contested position, clear out the remaining opposition, take and hold the ground. He seeks out the enemy in his hiding place and with rifle, bayonet, hand grenade or bare hands wrings final surrender from the enemy soldier. In the final stages, the infantryman goes alone. He does the job by himself; succeeds or fails by his own efforts. It is a man-to-man, kill-or-be-killed proposition. He moves in and takes the ground. If he fails, then the Air Corps and the artillery and the tankers fail. If he succeeds, all other arms succeed and another little patch of ground, another pillbox, another hill is added to the sum total of victory. War is never on a grand scale. It is a composite of little battles for bridges, road junctions, houses and even single machine gun emplacements. To the men engaged in these individual struggles, these little battles are the most important of all for their lives are at stake in the outcome. The foxhole occupied by one doughboy is the most important hole in all the world, because he is in it. The successes or failures in all the little battles, added up, means victory or defeat in the final analysis. Without the infantry all other arms and services would be useless. In back of the infantryman are all the support weapons and supplies so necessary for war. In front of him there is "nothing but the enemy".

'War is never glamorous. War is a dirty, filthy business. It is life lived under the most miserable conditions. It is death suffered under the most horrible circumstances. It is fought on lonely hillsides, in rubbled towns, in ditches and sewers and cellars, in rain, and snow and mud, in pain and fear. War is training and marching, privation and lack of individual privacy, work and sweat and loneliness, periods of long waiting, short battles, endless patrolling, enemy planes that strafe highways, the whistle of enemy shells, cold rations and foot blisters, life stripped to its barest essentials. War is dead men in the hot sun, dying men screaming in pain, wrecked men in hospitals with plates in their skulls, sightless eyes, stumps of legs and arms, men fed through tubes or with their insides held together by wire. War is men with shattered minds in padded cells. War is men who wake up in the middle of the night, shaking and screaming, and then realise they're waking from a dream. War is people saying endless goodbyes – is women waiting, and some not waiting – is men returning and telegrams which read that "The War Department regrets . . ." – is "Welcome Home" or "I don't want you". War is something that should never happen, but does. War is the most awful, the most unforgettable experience a man could have. War in the infantry is all that and more. There is no "glamour in the infantry". You learn how much blood you have to pay for 50-odd yards of battle-scarred mud, In the infantry, there are no crash helmets, no fancy wings for the girls back home to wear. You're just a guy with a gun, and a job to do!'

* For American readers, this may need explaining, being a British World War I term standing for: 'Poor Bloody Infantry'.

The second description was written by a British infantry soldier – my good friend James Lucas, who served with the 1st Battalion of the Queen's Own Royal West Kent Regiment in North Africa and with the Queen's Royal West Surrey Regiment in Italy as part of Fifth Army. A distinguished historian, who has written many books himself, he has very kindly allowed me to quote from his own story about his army days which has not yet been published (interested publishers please note!). This is how he describes facing a German attack:

'Fortunately I never experienced a German assault larger than that of company size, and despite my fears I never ceased to have compassion for the enemy. The soldiers seemed so naked and vulnerable, their line seemed to be so small, the countryside through which they were attacking was so vast and the resources of the Imperial Army against which they were pitting their insignificant strength so irresistible, that their attack seemed to have more the nature of a forlorn hope than to offer any chance of success. The first indication, apart from the almost mandatory bombardment, was usually a series of short, sharp thrusts to probe the weak points of the defence and then, with a dramatic suddeness which was always disconcerting, groups of men would rise up from the ground and begin to move towards our positions. It never seemed that they were running – they appeared to cover the ground with a smooth, gliding motion, for they either wore greatcoats or else the growing crops through which they were advancing concealed the movement of their feet and lower legs. They carried their weapons almost as if they were an integral part of themselves, shaking and gesticulating with them as they came forward. We carried our guns as if they were tools, casually, from long familiarity, but with care. Although it always looked as if the enemy advanced in a single line, in effect they were invariably deployed tactically and their assaults were skilfully supported by machine gun fire and artillery fire.

'Almost as soon as we sighted them they would disappear into dead ground and now would come the testing time for us. Tensely we would brace ourselves against the parapets of our small trenches, shuffling our elbows in the loose soil to make a more secure or more comfortable rest for the weapon pressed into our shoulders. All around us – before us – behind us – shells and mortar bombs, unheralded by the whistle which preceded artillery shot, would explode with crashing detonations and complementing the vicious bombardment would be the wi-wip-wip of bullets as machine guns traversed across our positions. Heads and torsos unprotected from this rain of metal, magazines charged, grenades to hand, sights set at 200yd, buffeted by a tornado of enemy fire, we would wait patiently for the Germans to appear from the ground into which they had disappeared. Our company officers, completely exposed to the barrage, would walk about in the open, moving from position to position encouraging, calming and supporting their men.

'The distance at which the Jerries made their last run in varied according to the ground but they never seemed to grow in the normal fashion. From the time of their first being seen they seemed to become neither bigger, nor to get nearer until, like the appearance of the Demon King in pantomime, almost in the twinkling of an eye, there they would be – enormously tall, monstrously wide, bellowing and shouting, the weapons in their hands seemed to give out burst of liquid fire, while their bodies and arms moved gracefully and elegantly through a series of arcs as they projected their hand grenades upon our defensive line. Tensely we would await the order to fire, and it was always with a feeling of relief that this would come, but it was alarming to discover that the soldier whose chest the foresight had been covering, had not fallen when the trigger was squeezed and that,

Below: A medic applies a triangular bandage to the head wound of an infantry soldier in the Mignano sector./US Army

despite the intensity of our fire, the enemy was visibly closing in. The very air was a hubbub of noise for, although by now the artillery fire had stopped and the explosions of grenades would be the loudest detonation, streams of bullets which criss-crossed the area made a whooshing sound like running water and from our attacking enemy would come a bellowing ''oorah, oorah''. All around there would be the shouts of the wounded, calls for the stretcher bearers, screams from those mortally hit, curses and shrieks and usually a thumping sound of a Bren gunner's hand trying to bang clear a stoppage which had caused the gun to cease firing at a critical moment. In all this pandemonium the lessons of fire discipline, so painfully learnt on a barrack square in Blighty, would prove themselves and, almost by instinct, rifles would be reloaded, aim taken and pressures applied upon the trigger.

'Then, if we beat them off, quite suddenly they would be gone. In front of our slits there would be the dead, like bundles of old clothes. Among the wounded there was always one who sat on the ground, his face in his hands, rocking backwards and forwards and crying hysterically. Two of three wounded would be standing arms raised, chests heaving with exhaustion, their eyes drained empty of emotion, while down the slopes of the hill several small figures, jinking desparately from right to left, would be flying away covering the ground in that liquid, gliding motion. With the enemy's departure a reaction would set in and we would find ouselves exhausted and trembling, with no sense of elation at our victory, just a numbing lethargy from which the inevitable stonk could not rouse us and we responded only to the peremptory orders of our officers and NCOs, their curt commands restoring us, once again, to a realisation of our position. Then, true to Kipling's words: ''You do your work on water'', a quick pull on the bottle and oh, the delight of that first puff on a cigarette.

'It was always remarkable how, after an unsuccessful attack, the German mortar crews seemed to achieve a greater accuracy and how there was always a marked increase in sniper activity. Ted* always became quite bloody-minded in defeat or failure!'

* 'Ted' is short for the Italian word *Tedeschi* meaning German.

Below: The battle for Mte Camino. After the capture of Roccamonfina and Camino, Fifth Army found they had two new mountains to conquer. Two heights on Mte Marrone, part of the dominating high ground which overlooked the Capua-Rome road, were successfully captured. Photo shows men of the 46th and 56th Divisions passing through San Clemente, 6 December 1943./IWM

Finally in this short tribute to the infantry soldier is an article from that ever popular soldiers' newspaper *Yank*, which was entitled 'Counter-attack' and began with the byline: 'by Sgt Newton H. Fulbright, *Yank* Field Correspondent, with the Fifth Army in Italy'. It read:

'A hero is a damn fool, as any soldier in the frontline Infantry will tell you; a reckless guy can die in a minute in the shellfire in the Bowling Alley [GI name for the narrow twisting valley through which threads Highway 6, the principal road from Naples to Rome]. Yet once in a while a guy gets to be a sort of hero and lives to fight again. There were heroes like that in our push on San Pietro, the first objective in the Fifth Army's campaign to reduce the strong enemy positions in and around Cassino. The night my outfit piled over a mountain ridge to open the drive we lost so many men under concentrated mortar and artillery fire in the first few hours that we were literally stunned. We dug in to hold what we had. Our position was precarious. We were seriously strained for manpower to outpost our positions facing the enemy on an indefinite front, extending from barren, towering rocks on our right to the open, shell-plowed valley below us on the left. We sat there for the next few days, nervously feeling the Jerry out, blasting away with our artillery and being blasted in turn by his. We renewed the attack, supported this time by tanks. The sound and the fury was terrific, greater than anything thought up by Orson Welles, but we got absolutely nowhere. Then the Jerry attacked. It came about dark on the tenth day. I was sitting in the company CP when the German machine guns began chattering down the road. "Counter-attack!" There was no need for anyone to shout the warning. Already soldiers were dashing to shooting positions on the double; telephones and radios were busy calling down artillery fire.

'The line to our mortar platoon on the hill went out with the first crash of enemy artillery. I dived out of the CP and began threading my way up the hill, amid the crash of shells, toward the positions. Added to the noise was the cry of the wounded, thrashing and stumbling in the dark, pleading for help to get them to the aid station. The plight of the wounded is always a strain on the nerves of the unwounded soldier. He wants to help; his instinct is to stop and give aid. But he hasn't time; he must keep going. At that moment I heard our 81s begin firing. I recognised the voice of a soldier in the dark who was calling for a medic. I went up to him. "I've been hit," he said. "They got me in the back with a hand grenade. They crawled up to a wall and tossed it right into my foxhole. It blew me out." Fully a dozen walking wounded had come up. It was only a little way to the aid station. We started out. I gave support to my friend who had been hit by the potato masher. One of his legs was dragging. "I think they got me in the kidney," he said. Our first mortar position was located a short distance up from a little draw. I found so many empty mortar cases around the position that I had to crawl on my hands and knees to get to the gun. Cpl Quinten Barrington of Hubbard, Texas, was standing beside the gun with a round in his hand. "What kind of a position you got here?" I asked. We are always uneasy about our mortars. Jerry always tries for mortar positions. "I got one of the Germanese positions", said Cpl Barrington, with shell poised over the mortar barrel. "They can't get me out of it." Wham! and another round was on the way. The counter-attack didn't last long after that. Cpl Barrington was certainly one of the heroes I mentioned when I began this piece; but you'll never hear him admit it. "I put my No 1 man aside. I've been carrying that barrel longer than he has," he explained. "I've waited for four years to blow the soot out of that barrel. It was well blown out tonight."

'We checked up later and found that Cpl Barrington had fired better than 200 rounds while the enemy shells burst so close around him that most of the platoon kept giving him up for lost – until they heard his gun again. The counter-attack was definitely over by 2300 hours, and I made my way through the lines. I ran into 1st Sgt Red Jones of another company (Nobody ever calls him anything but Red). "We've got a man who did some very good work here", Red told me. "Sgt Dudley Henry of Waco, Texas, took over the only mortar – a 60mm – that we had in the company. The best we can figure is that he fired between 800 and 1,000 rounds. We just know that it was better than 800, which ought to be some kind of record for one evenings' work." For my money it is. Talking with some of the boys, I learned more about this feat. The mortar barrel seems to have gummed up sometime during the evening. There was no cleaning material but this didn't stop Sgt Henry. He yanked off his shoes, slipped off his socks, ripped a limb from a nearby olive tree, swabbed the barrel out with this improvised contraption and went back to work.

'There are a lot more heroes, but you get the idea. It's guts, probably – you need a lot of guts up here in the Bowling Alley. The next morning Jerry had pulled out and left. We found him about nightfall, though, he was over near San Vittore waiting for us, and the game went on with little, if any, interruption.'*

* From *Yank*, The Army Weekly and published here by kind permission of the Office of the Chief of Public Affairs, Department of the Army, Washington DC.

Cutting the Winter Line

During the two and a half months following the Salerno landings, Fifth Army had advanced from the beaches northwards through the autumn rains and mud. They had cleared Naples, crossed the Volturno and their advance had now slowed in front of the German defences known as the Winter Line, which comprised a belt of well fortified hills and passes, protecting the even more formidable Gustav Line. Progress was difficult, with the weather and terrain favouring the defenders in their well protected dugouts, from which they were able to produce accurate machine gun and mortar fire over the mine studded approaches. Fifth Army HQ was at this time located in an enormous Bourbon palace at Caserta, and was busy planning an operation to commit two of its three corps in an assault, in early December, against the strong German positions. British 10 Corps was on the sea flank (ie to the west) faced with the capture of Monastery Hill, Monte Camino and the forcing of a crossing over the lower Gargliano. US II Corps was up against the eastern slopes of Monte Camino – la Difensa – Monte Maggiore hill mass. For 12 days they had tried to gain this ground, but had failed with heavy casualties. US VI Corps was on the right, engaged in a series of small actions, with the 45th Division probing beyond the upper Volturno around Pozzili and their Rangers held up just beyond Venafro. They would shortly be relieved by the French Expeditionary Corps.

Although relatively unsophisticated when compared with the Todt organisation-built Gustav Line, the Winter Line was still a formidable obstacle, particularly as there was no single key position (like Cassino) which presented the attacker with the opportunity to break the entire system with one bold stroke. Each of the sucessive defensive positions had to be taken, each valley cleared. Added to this were the hardships of knee deep, axle deep mud – 'foxhole engulfing mud' as someone described it. Fifth Army soldiers had insufficient winter kit as yet issued with which to combat the rain, snow, cold and sleet of this their first taste of Italian winter. Trucks bogged down in the soupy ground, machine gun barrels froze solid, shoes wore out in a single day on the sharp rocks, whilst howitzer trails just wouldn't stay dug in – one round and the guns buried themselves.

Against this background of lousy weather, difficult terrain and strong enemy positions, I have chosen two stories of action by units of Fifth Army. Both were, as we will see, part of the Fifth Army's assault on the Winter Line, which was called, appropriately, Operation Raincoat. The first features a unique American/Canadian unit, known as 'The Braves'; the second, 2/5th Queens of 56 British Infantry Division.

Below: Map 2 Operation Raincoat, 2-9 December 1943.

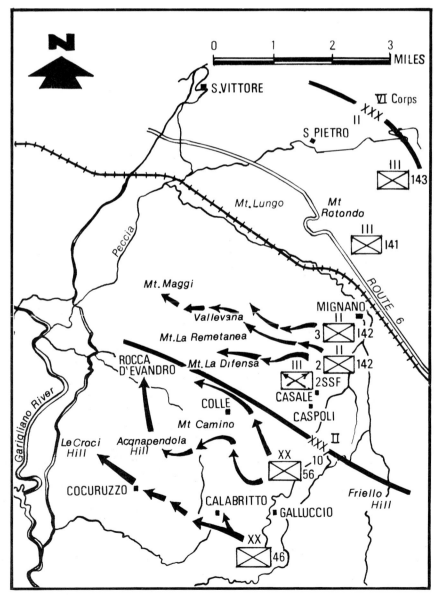

Above: Defenders of the Winter Line. Two 'gefreiters' (lance corporals) move into an observation post to relieve their comrades. The rear one appears to be carrying a small cable drum, presumably for line communications back to the main position./IWM

Above right: GIs bail out their AA gun emplacement in the Capua sector of the Fifth Army front. From the rear view under its cover the gun looks to be a .50 Browning./US Army

Centre right: American engineers have to deal with flood waters on the Volturno River, north of Venafro, the photo shows them lashing the steel treads of this pontoon bridge to prevent them being swept away. /US Army

Bottom right: Mud, mud, glorious mud! Pack mules of an Italian Pack Mule Company supporting Fifth Army make better progress than wheeled transport, as winter rains turn the mountain tracks into quagmires./IWM

34

Above: US AA gunners in
the San Pietro area
prepare to engage enemy
aircraft with their half
track mounted multiple
mount which comprised
two .50 machine guns
mounted with a 37mm
gun./US Army

Left: The message on the
side of this shell tells its
own story, as US gunners
support Operation
Raincoat, December 1943.
/US Army

The Braves Take la Difensa

The Germans called them 'The Black Devils', outsiders 'The Bow and Arrow Boys', to each other they were simply 'The Braves' and their unit 'The Force'. Its official title was actually the 'First Special Service Force' – a title which often caused them to be confused with the US Forces entertainment branch! They consisted of volunteers from both USA and Canada, who were between the ages of 21 and 35, had three or more years of grammar school education, and came from the occupational range of lumberjacks, hunters, forest rangers, northwoodsmen, game wardens, prospectors and explorers. It is immediately apparent from this list of occupations that 'The Braves' were a very special force, trained in the arts of living under difficult conditions, able to ski, to climb mountains, and to parachute into action whenever needed. Their first major action was the attack and capture of a hill feature known as la Difensa during six bloody days

in early December 1943. Before describing part of this action, it may be useful if I give a few more details about the Force which was unique within Fifth Army. It was composed of three regiments, each commanded as normal by a full colonel. However, each had a strength of only 32 officers and 385 men (the enlisted strength was later increased by 50%). Regiments were divided into two battalions, with three companies in each of three platoons per company. Platoons were broken down into two sections, the basic fighting unit throughout the Force. Each of the 12-man sections could be equipped with four Weasels – a light tracked vehicle, specially designed for winter warfare – when required, and was armed with an assortment of light weapons including a Browning machine gun, a 60mm mortar, a portable flame thrower and a Johnson LMG. The latter, obtained from the US Marines in exchange for a quantity of a very special new explosive called 'RS' of which the Force were the sole army users, was in preference to the

Below: Map 3 1 SSF attack on La Difensa, 2-8 December 1943.

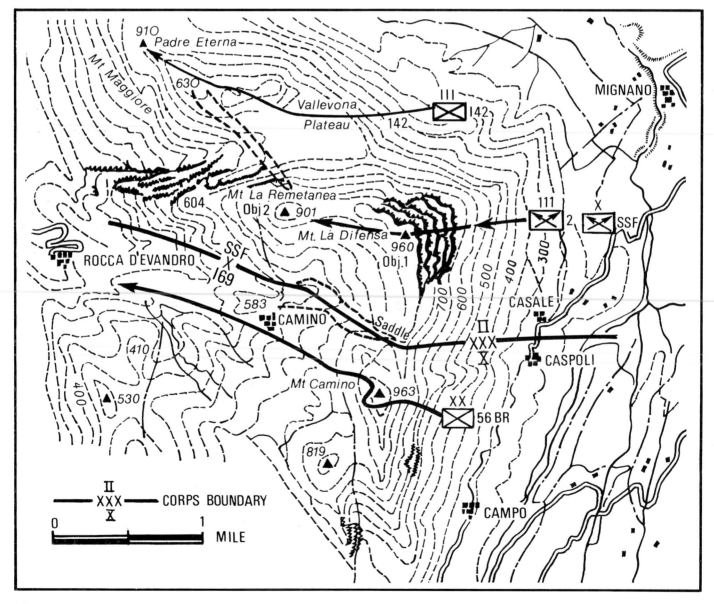

Right: Members of 'The Force' prepare for a raid behind enemy lines./*IWM*

Below: Medical supplies move up by mule to an infantry first aid station in the mountains./*US Army*

Bottom: Ground crews of the USAAF load auxiliary fuel tanks with food and medical supplies. They are then placed in the bomb racks of an A-36A Mustang aircraft and dropped to Fifth Army troops fighting high on the slopes of Mte Maggiore, near Mignano. /*USAAF*

Browning Automatic Rifle (BAR). Being only slightly heavier than an M1 rifle, but with a firepower better than the BAR, it was ideal for a light, fast moving combat unit. But the Force did lack the normal heavy weapons found in the standard infantry battalion. Their cap badge (crossed arrows), had once been the insignia of the inactivated Indian Scouts. It is little wonder that these tough, highly individualistic soldiers sometimes fell foul of those in authority, as Col Robert D. Burhans explains in his excellent book about the Force: 'One of the Braves (whilst on Christmas leave) found himself in Salt Lake City and was accosted by a squad of military police who told the Forceman he was out of uniform because he didn't have leggings and wore his trousers tucked into his parachute boots. Utah was a long way from Fort Benning;* the parachute uniform was not in the catalog of the military police in those parts. So the military police sought to enforce their orders by requiring the man from Helena to "pull those pants outa yer boots!" "Where I come from that's the uniform. If you want to take them out you can try," the man from Helena shot back. The MPs felt safe in their numbers and moved in to do their duty.

'In short order, by competent use of vicious groin kicks and eye punches, the parachutist had four military police on the ground. In the end, several MPs, a few of them temporarlly incapacitated, had pulled out the trousers and bundled the non-reg soldier off to head-

* The base for the Force was at Fort William Harry Harrison, an unused National Guard Post in the rugged mountains of Montana, near Helena. Fort Benning was a parachute training centre which the Force used for their para training.

quarters. A search of records uncovered the fact that there was such a unit in Montana, with such a uniform, and to the MPs' chagrin, the man was entirely in order.'

The Force's attack on la Difensa was, as I have mentioned, part of Fifth Army's Operation Raincoat which took place 1-11 December 1943. The Force had moved up from Naples on November 21 to occupy an Italian artillery barracks at Santa Maria (Capua-Vetere) which had been recently evacuated by the Hermann Göring Panzer Division headquarters:
'. . . on their departure before the onrushing Fifth they had broken their lease by demolishing all washrooms and kitchens. Living quarters were slightly less wrecked, and if the first view suggested Roman ruins, a later look proved the base a better home than the canvas then housing everyone else.'

After normal recces, briefings etc, all carried out in the incessant rain of late November, D-Day was set for 28 November, but then had to be put back to the 29th, then the 30th and finally to 1 December, because of the impossibility of providing air support in the appalling weather conditions. The first of December was a bright morning and from the top floors of the barracks at Santa Maria it was possible to look across the snow covered peaks of the Apennines to the main ridge that separated the Fifth and Eighth Armies, whilst towards the sea 'one could observe the sharp brow of Mt la Difensa clearly visible with its light fall of snow'. At 1600 hours the Second Regiment loaded into transport and moved out, followed by the First and then the Third at hourly intervals. Col Burhans takes up the story:
'It was dark when they arrived at Presenzano near the 36th Division command post where the men would detruck and march the 10 miles to their position. A light rain was falling when the first trucks came in at 9.00 o'clock. The heavy gloom and the rain reflected the flashes of the 155s picking up their nightly harassing missions from positions behind the road. The men went through their usual profane detrucking into the roadside mud, and started off with a semblance of order. For Second Regiment, guides tried to take a map short cut off the selected route, but the mire was knee-deep through the olive orchards. A heavy battle pack made such slogging extremely tiring. By midnight the column cut over to Conca and proceded more easily up the road through the flickering light in the zone of the lighter artillery. First and Third Regiments came down the road all the way. It was a cold wet night through which the long column of men slipped and plowed and swore to the base of the hill. When the sharp ravines were reached it was nearly 3.00am. The rain stopped and the Second Regiment toiled on up and settled itself in the scrub pine cover halfway up Difensa. As the last man closed into the bracken, dawn broke, and the sun came up on a well-secreted Second.'

The other two regiments, who were not committed to the first assault, had also taken cover up and down the length of the ravine and were well asleep. But they were not to sleep for long as there was much to do.
'We awoke to a bright sun covering the eastern slope of Difensa with a brilliant green. It towered above us making our raw, narrow ravine seem like a scratch in the ground. The rain had mired this yellow clay wadi into a rich bottomless slough. Its course seemed to go toward Mignano draining down into the Pescia further down. The men were already up, cooking breakfast on the mountain stoves, trying to find a dry spot to throw their shelter halves. It was a place well within enemy observation, for the day previous enemy mortar and machine gun fire had worked up and down its length at intervals to say nothing of a strafing and bombing visit from friendly aircraft.
'The day wore on. Shortly after noon Second Regiment, resting secreted in the scrub pine cover along the 400-metre line halfway up Difensa, slowly stirred in the warm sun. There were occasional individual actions of men about to enter battle; honing fighting knives, retaping hand grenades, checking ammunition, scattered bull sessions. About 4.00 o'clock word came around to eat the cold K rations and get ready to move out. Most officers had not slept, being busy with reconnaissances and supply details.
'Dusk came early. Clouds blotted out the sun before setting. Linemen brought in the wire leading from Hill 368* and runners reported variously that Second was moving up. First Regiment was on the move to its reserve position and 1st Battalion, Third Regiment was heading for the 600-metre assembly area to be employed in the event of trouble. With the last light ended the incessant droning of planes. The long Camino-Difensa ridge became a soft grey blur through rising fog. From sporadic concentrations laid on the mountain throughout the day the artillery increased its tempo along the ridge after dark. By 10.00pm there was a continuous window-shade rustle overhead, with a faraway whine that crept down from the mountain top. A murderous seething and crackling thundered along the Camino-

* Gen Wilbur's HQ was located on Hill 368 – the Force had been assigned to 36 Division for the operation and Gen Wilbur was the Asst Div Comd 36 Division.

Difensa ridge. The batteries along the road behind the command post were firing four and six guns at a time.

'In the high gloom troops were filing slowly up the mountain trails. This was the heaviest concentration of artillery in the Italian campaign thus far, perhaps the heaviest of the war. By 10.30 Second Regiment had reached the base of the Difensa crown. Supporting artillery fires were slackening off in intensity while increasing range to cover the second objective. At the same time enemy batteries, earlier reported withdrawing toward Cassino, were working up and down the known supply trails as if sensing our approach. The 142nd's trails to the north and the Force's routes up the east side were feeling strong 105mm and 155mm fire. Heavier calibres – the long ranging 170s – were thumping into congested artillery positions stretched behind the forward roads. Halfway up Difensa in the Force sector and somewhat toward the British side of the line, an enemy machine pistol man was "pointing" mortar fires with machine pistol tracer. He fired on a 15 minute schedule. After each tracer burst, mortar bursts from the heights would drop near the supply caves at the broken bridge, the command post in the gulley, even the aid station behind the road.

'Day had ended in a thick bank of darkening clouds. Now the night was pitch black. By midnight the heights were invisible from below. Slowly Col Williamson's Second Regiment worked in double file of companies of heavily laden men up the rope scramble in the order 1, 2, 3 Companies. After that it was 350yd to the peak over a steep rocky slope. Three o'clock came; 1 Company formed into skirmishers and set off. Still no enemy had been met head on but toward the top a machine pistol man was directing bursts down the mountain. He was also blind that night; the rounds were snapping high overhead. 1 Company moved out and it was something short of an hour later when 3 Company was off the ropes and squared away. Capt Rothlin's points reported back at 4.30am that the crest was just ahead. Battalion ordered 1 Company to flank leftward which it did while Capt Waters' 2 Company came abreast in the centre. Too many rocks rolled on this manoeuvre which was right on the doorsill of the enemy's forward positions. Surprise had been gained sufficiently by the battalion before the mortar rounds struck, then the machine gun curtain came down, finally sniper shots and the German positions were thoroughly awake. The sky became a blaze of red, green and illuminating flares. Capt Daugherty's 3 Company was flanking right to complete the assault disposition when 1 Company on the left started in.

'The automatic breakdown of battle put immediate command first in the platoon leaders' hands then further down, when sections had been fully committed, into the section leaders' hands. Finally, 18 sections in the battalion, fully oriented on plan and objective, were involved with their own individual problems and plans and techniques of tightening and advancing the battalion crescent to the height of Hill 960. From 5.00am it would be still an hour to daylight with a dense cloud even then blanketing out visibility. Each company's light mortars had gone into handy defile behind rocks or in shallow gullies. The light machine guns moved up in short jumps sited to cover the advancing riflemen. In the darkness and confusion before daylight the first casualties were calling for aid men or stumbling to the rear for treatment. Light broke as 1 Company had consolidated to within 100m of the peak. Advanced sections were well engaged with the main enemy defence bastion on this height, a complex of caves and pillboxes built to support mutually by fixed fires. By using ropes and advancing on the north-east quadrant of the mountain the assaulting force had overcome the initial German disposition of defences covering the easier terrain approaches from the north and east. Advantage number one. By employing the skill and stamina trained into them, and the natural energy God gave them, the men had seized swiftly the profits of the first advantage and turned it into a second advantage. The heavy howitzer concentrations which earlier in the evening seemed to be pulverising the mountain had barely cracked the hard limestone of la Difensa. Within the solid construction of their pillboxes the Germans waited.

'With the light came a chance for the scouts to move out at effective distances concealed in the fog. In the 2 Company zone Sgt McGinty had started his section on a right flanking move as part of the platoon job to knock out the final crest defense of the enemy. On top the Germans had six heavy machine guns emplaced to cover the northen approaches. Hastily their pieces swung on the advancing 2nd Company; as the Germans improved their positions on the higher ground and brought up 12 machine pistol men to snipe, Sgt McGinty's section began losing men fast. Sgts Van Ausdale and Fenton who had led the company up from the assembly area as advance points, saw the section's position and swung to the left flank where they both delivered automatic fire on the enemy until the McGinty section could remove its wounded. In the hour's soirée men had become detached from units. Pinned down, they waited leaderless for reorganisation. Sgt Van Ausdale gathered up eight such men, ordered a nearby machine gun team to lay down fire, called for three mortar rounds from the company emplacement and led his improvised section over the ledge in straight assault on the first cave. Grenades and bayonets got the first cave and the same instruments dispatched the second gun a bit further up.

'On the left of the assaulting battalion, 1 Company was undertaking to clean up a ridge supporting part of the heavy machine gun complex on the peak of Difensa. As Lt Kaasch led his platoon into the gloom two more enemy machine guns were rattling to the front with such volume that he ordered the platoon onto a firing line for support. Taking two men he advanced on the guns. Caught on the flank the first gun crew surrendered intact; similar tactics caught the second crew still firing when a few grenades effectively silenced the gun. Few enemy were found alive. The gathering light and successful advance started to yield up prisoners walking in with hands in the air. The steady drive of 1 Company had placed them near the top. One German started across a gully waving a white flag. Capt Rothlin went out of his cover to receive the prisoner. Immediately the German dropped into a hole and his squad concealed in the rear opened up full out on the Captain. He fell without a sound. The nearest section of 1 Company quickly despatched the decoy, then rushed the cover and accounted for several more Germans. Lt Piette took command. For one minute the fog parted as if fate was giving the battalion a chance to look at its handiwork. 1 and 2 Companies were on top of Difensa which appeared to be a shallow saucer depression hemmed in by a circling ridge. Straight to the west the ridge declined slightly to la Remetanea (Hill 907, the second objective). Farther down the ridge Germans were seen swarming like ants toward the valley and the next hill. Mortars were called for fire and the rounds were in the air when the cloud closed back covering observation of the bursts. By 7.00am all the 1st Battalion had mounted the hill. LTC Moore soon arrived at the head of the 2nd Battalion in the support role ready to take over the hill while LTC MacWilliam's men were released for the rest of the eminence. Another hour's consolidating remained, to clean out remaining snipers, reorganise the sections, platoons, and companies, and to dig in against the inevitable counter-attack.'

Of course that vivid description of the Force's initial assault on la Difensa was only the beginning of an exceptionally hard fought and difficult battle, set in appalling conditions with rain, fog and ice all sapping the energy of the attackers. Add to this the discomforts of no shelter, insufficient blankets, cold food, fatigue and the continual mortaring and shelling, and one can well appreciate the hardships which the Braves suffered. The Force handed

over its hard won positions on la Difensa and la Remetanea at the end of six cold, bloody days. Their total casualties in the operation were 511 – 73 killed, 9 missing, 313 wounded or injured and 116 exhaustion cases.

Monte Camino

In the British 10 Corps sector arrangements were going on, in step with the la Difensa operations, for the assault on Monte Camino. In brief the plan was that 46 Division would first attack the Calabritto spur which ran up to the mountain from the south-west. The 56th Division would then assault the main feature in several phases viz: 167 Brigade would attack 'Bare' Ridge from the south, while 169 Brigade assaulted 'Razor Back' from the east. The final assault on the Monastery summit would be made by either brigade, depending upon the situation. 168 Brigade and 201 Guards Brigade would both be in reserve for future operations. We will follow the fortunes of 2/5th Queens who were part of 169 Brigade. They were to assault the

Right: Preparations for Operation Raincoat. The infantry, well laden, begin their advance, 1 December 1943./*IWM*

Below right: The battle for Mte Camino. Looking across at the mountain from a rock sangar held by the R Hants./*IWM*

Below: Map 4 The Battle of Monte Camino, 2-5 December 1943.

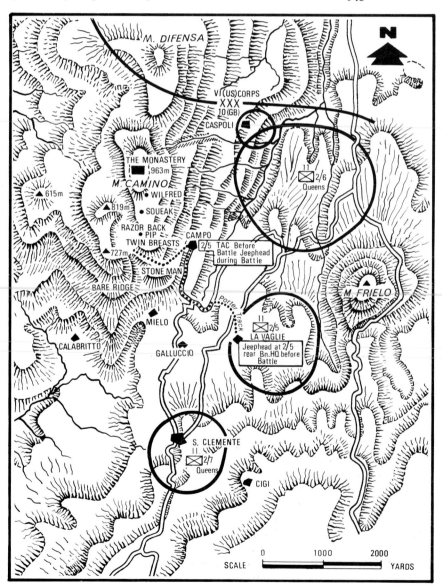

Razor Back via the 'Twin Breasts' – an aptly named feature on the way up to the three clearly defined pimples of Razor Back which were codenamed 'Pip', 'Squeak' and 'Wilfred' (after three comic strip characters in English childrens' comic papers). Whilst this attack was taking place the 2/6th Queens would make a diversionary attack with one company towards the saddle north of the Monastery feature. The remainder of the 2/6th and the whole of the other battalion in the brigade, the 2/7th, would act as porters for the attacking troops. No barrage would be possible owing to the steepness of the slope, so it was decided to support the climb by a series of what were called 'Terror crashes' in which artillery, mortars and machine guns would join in pulverising a small area which contained a known or suspected enemy position. These 'crashes' would then lift and return (usually three times) at irregular intervals.

During the build up before the attack patrolling was stepped up – this in itself required the utmost nerve and endurance,

41

involving a climb up the 3,000ft mountain, with only a gas cape and jerkin as protection against the bitter weather. By D-Day, all the attacking company and platoon commanders and many of the section commanders as well, had been up the mountain to see their objectives, often from a distance of less than 100yd. Many enemy posts were pinpointed and the habits of their occupants carefully studied. A South African officer, Capt C. D. Griffiths, seconded to the 2/5th, actually held an arms inspection in a German position while its garrison were temporarily away at breakfast! The other main preparation was the establishing of advanced bases as near as possible to the base of the climb. The 2/5th advanced base was Campo, whilst the 2/6th chose Caspoli which was already an established patrol base. Campo village was about 100ft up the slope, nestling snugly against it. By day no movement was allowed, as both bases were in full view of the monastery, but by night a stream of porters with rucksacks and Everest packs trudged the two miles up from the 2/5th Tactical HQ at La Vaglie. Ammunition, ration sacks and all types of stores were collected in the villages and the inhabitants

Above: The battle for Mte Camino. Bringing a casualty down from the mountains./IWM

Left: Operation Raincoat. Men of the supporting mortar companies of 138 Brigade (R Berks) marching through San Clemente towards the lower slopes of Mte Camino./IWM

Below left: Supporting fire. A Vickers .303in machine gun hammering away in support of the attack. Entering service in 1912, the Vickers was still in use in the mid-1970s! It had a rate of fire of 450-500rpm, was water cooled and fired a 250-round fabric belt./IWM

Right: Coming off the mountain. Men of the Queens move down Mte Camino after their successful attack./IWM

were sworn to secrecy – which they faithfully observed.

A week before D-Day – set for 2 December – platoons and sections moved by night into billets in the forward bases, where no one was allowed to show himself, and by day observation had to be through shaded windows. The night of the 2nd was still and dark until the guns opened fire:

'They did so with dramatic suddenness, the quiet being broken by the terrific crashes, reverberating like thunder from the mountainsides, while the ground and sky were lit up like day, the pink tracer of the Bofors being especially striking. It was said to be the greatest bombardment since Alamein.'*

Great fragments from the higher slopes, plus the inevitable 'drop shorts' began falling close to the waiting troops as they began their climb. It was very steep, uneven going, over a mixture of tall tufty grass, rocks and loose stones, all too easy to overbalance under the weight of a huge rucksack and blanket. D Company, 2/5th had the furthest to go and

* History of the Queen's Royal Regiment, Vol VIII; compiled by Major R.C.G. Foster, MC.

left their rucksacks at Campo, but everyone else had to carry their own as there were not enough porters. After about five hours climbing there was a halt at the 'Stone Man' – a prominent stone pillar about four feet high which formed a splendid landmark. Rucksacks were dumped there, pockets filled with ammunition and bayonets fixed. D Company under Capt C. D. Griffiths then climbed to the assault – they were a specially formed company made up of the carrier and mortar platoons. As with the American assault on la Difensa, the enemy remained unaware of the attackers until they were very close, when at last a sentry above them shouted the alarm. Grenades and bursts of Spandau fire now echoed among the rocks. 16 Platoon went on scrambling straight up, while 18 Platoon moved around to clear the caves behind. Fighting was very confused and it was difficult to get at the Germans who held the higher ground. By midnight C Company, commanded by Capt P. M. Bramwell, were well up on the Pip pimple, but D had only a tenuous footing on Squeak. Lt J. D. Allison led his platoon in a determined assault on Squeak, but was mortally wounded and died

Below: Italian soldiers of the 1st Motorised Group, who were part of Fifth Army during the attack of the Winter Line, move up to the front.
/Stato Maggiore dell'Esercito

Bottom: Men of 1st Motorised Group advance up the rocky slopes of Mte Lungo. These Italian soldiers fought bravely for Fifth Army during the breaking of the Winter Line positions.
/Stato Maggiore dell'Esercito

whilst he was being carried down the mountain, but not before he had given his CO an exact account of the situation. At first light, the commanding officer, Lt-Col J. Y. Whitfield, led a platoon of D Company in a further assault and successfully captured Squeak. All around were other German posts, some fighting, some showing white flags and some just 'lying doggo'. The rest of D Company moved up onto Squeak and sent a patrol forward to Wilfred, which was heavily engaged. After subjecting Wilfred to a 45-minute barrage of fire, B Company passed through D and captured it. Razor Back was in British hands.

167 Brigade had taken Points 819 and 727, so the first phase of the attack was on the whole very successful. The diversion north of the monastery reached the saddle, but couldn't make further progress. Col Whitfield, realising that an early capture of the monastery was vital, decided to go for it even though his battalion had not yet been allocated it as an objective. A fighting patrol of A Company had already tried to reach it but had been beaten back, so he now sent a further patrol from B Company, under cover of the thick morning mist. On the way it was dispersed by heavy mortar fire. Its leader, Lt H. Lilley, actually reached the monastery, but was grenaded from the summit, some 30ft above and 10yd beyond. His ankle was shattered and he had to stay in a cave for the next 24 hours before being evacuated. B Company were now too exhausted by the bitter weather to make a further effort, so C Company was ordered to make a recce for an attack in the morning, with mortar and machine gun support and a smokescreen. The thick mist actually lasted throughout the morning of the 4th, so there was no need for the smokescreen and the attack by C Company went in on the monastery around noon. Under heavy fire the company reached the building itself, but found it impossible to get at the Germans on the hill behind, despite the distance only being some 20yd. The intervening space was bare rock about 12yd wide, with a sheer precipice on both sides. 13 and 14 Platoons tried to work around the flanks, but found it impossible, then 14 Platoon tried a head on advance up the rocky face in the centre, but lost their platoon commander, platoon sergeant and two section commanders. All this was taking place in a raging hailstorm, which numbed the fingers so that the men could only handle their weapons for a short while without relief. Capt Bramwell, OC C Company, finally ordered his men to stay on their side of the monastery wall and to cover the German positions. He was joined shortly by his CO and the commander of a company of the London Irish Rifles, who had been put under command for a final attack that night. It was clear that C Company had suffered too many casualties and was far too exhausted to do more than hold on to their present positions. A platoon of B Company was sent up to reinforce them, but lost all bar seven men on the way, from enemy fire. Unfortunately, the London Irish company lost its way in the pitch black night and so their attack never materialised, so next morning the position was still stalemated, with B Company relieving C in the monastery. Meanwhile, to the north of the monastery, C Company of the 2/6th had attacked the saddle and Pimple, but were caught in friendly defensive fire and had to withdraw with casualties.

That afternoon Lt-Col Whitfield decided to move a skeleton Tactical HQ into the monastery, including a gunner FOO (Forward Observation Officer). As they were approaching, the Germans put down heavy mortar fire, collapsing the roof of the monastery and wounding the company commander, Lt G. Hill. All his platoon commanders and his company sergeant major were casualties and he had only 20 men left. As he was briefing the CO and party, a shower of grenades fell on them and he was wounded again. The CO returned to Pip with his party where he was told that a company of the 2/7th was to be placed under his command and in fact it arrived that evening about 2100 hours. Plans were made for an attack the next morning, but these were countermanded by the Brigade Commander, who decided that the 2/7th would first take over from the badly mauled 2/5th. However, whilst 2/7th were still climbing up the mountain a white flag appeared on the top. A platoon of B Company 2/7th, already under command of the 2/5th, began to move up to accept the surrender, but when they were only halfway along the Razor Back feature, a friendly mortar concentration delayed them, so that by the time they were able to move on the area was completely empty of enemy apart from dead. While they were trying to escape the Germans were caught in the fire of 167 Brigade and wiped out. The whole mountain was now in the hands of the Queen's at long last. 2/5th were relieved by the 2/7th and moved down the mountain to rest, their casualties were 26 killed, 53 wounded and 19 missing. Two days later they buried their dead in an impressive funeral service at the monastery. Many months later the Moroccan Goums, themselves formidable mountain fighters, were training on Mte Camino and were so impressed by its strength and the feat of its capture that they erected a plaque: *Aux combattants Britanniques tombes glorieusement au Monte Camino*. A party of Russian generals also visited the battlefield and awarded the Order of the Red Star to Col Whitfield as a tribute to the bravery of his battalion.

Cassino — the Epic

The Battlefield

On both flanks the formidable Gustav Line was based upon a series of rivers and ridges which formed flexible defensive zones. In the centre, however, the line became far more rigid, fixed as it was on heavily fortified mountainous positions. The key to these positions lay in the wide valley of the River Liri, about 60 miles to the south-east of Rome. Here, the Matesi mountains towered above the surrounding area, commanding all possible approaches. Their highest point was Mte Cairo, some 5,000ft above the valley floor. From its side a spade-shaped promentory of high ground thrust down some 10 miles towards the valley of the Rapido River in the east and the Liri valley to the north east. This was the Monastery Hill massif. The little town of Cassino snuggled around its lower slopes, Route 6, one of the main routes joining Rome to Naples, snaked up from the south, crossed the Rapido, swung through Cassino and then turned north-west along the eastern side of the Liri valley. Despite the awesome size of Mte Cairo it was not the key to the area as it could be bypassed, but Monastery Hill was a very different matter. Nothing could traverse the Liri or the Rapido valleys without the consent of Cassino.

'Towering above precipitous slopes, as if in middle air, the great Benedictine hospice had been converted into a fortress in the 19th century. Even in the days of unlimited high explosive this lofty keep constituted a formidable obstacle. An imposing gate set in arches of stone thirty feet thick offered the only entrance. The walls were 15ft high, 10ft thick at their bases, loop-holed and tesselated. They were unscaleable and proof against any weapons which the infantry might bring to bear.'*

The first battle of Cassino had taken place in January 1944, when Fifth Army had launched three of its corps from three different sides, whilst a fourth landed at Anzio (see next chapter). The British 10th Corps were on the left, attacking below the junction of the Gari and Liri rivers, in order to bypass Cassino. In the centre, US II Corps launched a frontal assault across the Rapido river towards the high escarpments between Mte Cairo and Monastery Hill. On the right, the French Expeditionary Corps, driving from the north east, tried to infiltrate behind Mte Cairo. There were some gains on both flanks but the

* *The Tiger Triumphs;* published by HMSO for the Government of India, 1946.

Below: 5 Panorama of Cassino.

vital attack was in the centre, and it failed, despite the great gallantry of the American troops involved.

'Jo Hukam'

' "It was proper that we should have worn eagles upon our shoulders, for only birds could have visited so many lands, or could have soared to some of the places where we fought. We went first, and armies sprang up behind us. The tally of those we slew was likewise that of an army. We captured many lakhs of prisoners, and as they marched away, their columns stretched over the horizon. Of our men, we left the strength of two divisions upon our battlefields. *Jo Hukam.*"

'So will run the tale in a hundred villages, to the circle of elders and to the wide eyed children in the shade. Nor like many veterans' tales will it have grown unreasonably in stature. It is a matter of record that at one time 4th Indian Division was the only Allied infantry formation in the Mediterranean theatre. The "Game Book" of the Division, which kept the score of men, tanks, guns and aircraft, shows what a multiple toll it took; yet this one Division suffered over 25,000 casualties. It captured more than 100,000 prisoners, and in nine campaigns travelled more than 15,000 miles. Nevertheless such figures reveal less of the achievement of the 4th Indian Division than their proud phrase: "*Jo Hukam* – Whatever thing is required, that thing will we do."

'At the little town of Cassino, known to the military scholars as a model of impregnable terrain, an American corps, with gallantry beyond praise, had tried to storm the great buttress, which barred the way to Rome. Isloated, frozen, battered by night and by day, handfuls of indomitable men clung to positions which they had clawed from the grip of the enemy. When the Indians relieved these great soldiers, brigades barely mustered 400 men. Of one battalion only 50 men remained, and they were so spent that they had to be carried out on stretchers. Such was the fearful field to which 4th Indian Division was now committed. The desperate position in the Anzio bridgehead impelled high command to brook no delay. Brig Lovett's 7th Brigade was chosen to lead the way. The attack was planned to go in from the right flank, where the Americans had gained a footing on Snakes Head Ridge. Points 593 and 594 must be stormed before a startline could be established for the assault on the main objective – the mighty massif of Monastery Hill.

'On the night of 14 February the Royal Sussex surged against Point 593, to encounter paratroopers who fought with unequalled fanaticism and disregard of death in foxholes and weapon pits hidden among the rocks.

46

Left and centre left: The Monastery before and after. The old edifice was first bombed and shelled heavily on 15 February 1944 when 576 tons of bombs were dropped. The March attack, described here, was also preceded by a mammoth air strike – 1,140 tons of bombs being dropped by 338 heavy and 176 medium bombers. Subsequent attacks were also accompanied by similar air and artillery bombardment, until little of the original building remained./IWM

Bottom left: German officers assisting the Abbot of the Monastery of Monte Cassino into a car, before the destruction of the monastery by Allied bombing./IWM

Right: German paratroopers make good use of the ruins – this pair are manning a MG42, which was probably the best LMG of the war. Its high rate of fire produced a sound like tearing linoleum!/IWM

Below: Bombing of Cassino. A striking photo taken on 15 March 1944. /Alexander Turnbull Library, Wellington

Thrown back, the same battalion attacked the
next night and stormed their objective, but
through some misunderstanding were recalled. On the night of 17 February, 1/2
Gurkhas, 4/6 Rajputanas, 1/9 Gurkhas, with
the Rajputana Machine Gun Battalion in close
support, came forward and flung themselves at
the high ground. In a melee even fiercer than
Garci,* the Rajputanas took and lost Point
593. The Gurkha battalions swept forward
across minefields under an unparalleled blaze
of mortar bombs, grenades and spandau fire,
in a great bid to win the supreme prize of
Monastery Hill. Two thirds of the 1/2
Gurkhas were down in 10 minutes yet the
survivors battled on, leaving their dead far up
the slopes of the final objective. The attack
failed, for the task was more than men born of
women could encompass. Not only the
infantry and artillery (11 Field Regiment in
particular) paid toll in this maelstrom of
battle, every service lost heavily. During the
battle Subedar Subramanyan, a Madrassi
sapper, covered a mine with his body to save
his comrades and posthumously received the
George Cross.

'It was 15 March before a second attack
could be mounted. On that date 5th Brigade,
together with the New Zealand Division,
attempted to reach Monastery Hill by first
clearing the town of Cassino, which lay a
broken heap of masonry, in the shadow of the
great buttress. Once again fighting rose to a
crescendo of unbelieveable bitterness. The
Essex held Castle Hill, while 1/6th Rajputanas
joined the Kiwis in bitter and fluctuating

* Djebel Garci in Tunisia, where the Division
fought a hard battle in April 1943 during the
breakthrough to Tunis.

fighting on the lower slopes. Two nights later 1/9th Gurkhas won imperishable fame in one of the greatest exploits of the war. They stormed Hangman's Hill and for seven days and nights beat off the enemies who had closed in a ring around them. Those who lived were finally withdrawn when the operation was abandoned as hopeless. For the 4th Indian Division, as for many other fine divisions Cassino was Gethsemane.'

So runs the history of the 'Red Eagles' as it tells briefly of the part played by Fifth Army in the operations against Cassino. Operations which were not brought to a successful conclusion until it was finally attacked on 11 May 1944, by the Polish 2nd Corps, who, after weeks of terrible fighting took the ruined Monastery. I have chosen two actions in order to describe Fifth Army's part in the operations against Cassino, firstly the New Zealanders attack on Cassino town and Castle Hill, and secondly the holding of Hangman's Hill by the Gurkhas.

The Kiwis Attack

Gen Sir Bernard Freyberg, holder of the Victoria Cross from World War I, was commanding the New Zealand Corps in their assault on Cassino. A born fighter, Churchill likened him to a salamander because he 'thrived in fire', certainly his Corps was to have its fair share of 'fire' in their battle for the monastery. It was at his insistence that the monastery was bombed as a preliminary to the first NZ attack in February 1944. Much has been written about the rights and wrongs of this action. Those who supported it were convinced that the enemy had been using it for observation and other purposes (although

the Abbot-Bishop of Monte Cassino did sign a document certifying that no German troops were inside the monastery at the time of the air attack), those who were against it – and they included Mark Clark - were equally convinced that the bombing would merely make it an even more impregnable fortress. The monastery was heavily bombed and shelled on 15 February, with about 576 tons of bombs being dropped on and around the old building. When it was over the monastery building was almost completely destroyed, but the ruins that remained were even more useful to the German paratroopers. The bombing heralded a seres of relatively unsuccessful and extremely bloody assaults during the period 15-18 February by the New Zealand Corps. They were followed by a lull in the fighting until early March, while both sides licked their wounds and regrouped. Gen Freyberg had certainly not given up on Cassino and made fresh plans during the lull for another assault, this time from the direction of Cassino town, requiring the town and Castle Hill – Point 165 – Point 202 – Hangman's Hill, to be taken first. The attack was again preceded by massive air and artillery bombardments.

The objective of the 25th NZ Infantry Battalion was the western edge of Cassino from a point about 180yd north-east of the Castle to the road junction where the southern branch of Route 6 turned southwards at the Continental Hotel, thence 500yd east along Route 6 to the convent on the crossroads. Each of the leading companies had a troop of Shermans of B Squadron, 19 NZ Armoured Regiment attached. The advance was made along the two roads running south into the town (Caruso Rd and Parallel Rd – see map).

Crossing the start line at 1200 hours as the last of the bombers passed overhead, the Kiwis advanced behind a creeping barrage. There was practically no enemy fire to start off with, but the leading company came under small arms fire from Castle Hill as they were moving along the Rapido River – A Coy, the leading company, were actually in the river which was between 2-5ft in depth and very muddy. Progress was difficult and platoons became very spread out. The battalion history takes up the story:

'Under cover of the barrage and smokescreen the companies reached the town without much difficulty, and after deploying, gained their old positions level with the gaol without meeting the enemy. At this stage the two leading companies were in the same sectors as those taken over by them from the Americans, B Company on the right between the lower slopes of Castle Hill and the gaol, and A Company on the left from the gaol eastwards. When the companies advanced a little farther they soon encountered machine gun and rifle fire from Germans on the slopes of Castle Hill and in the ruins of the buildings on the flat. It was soon evident that overwhelming and devastating as the bombing and artillery barrage had appeared, they had not been able to destroy the enemy sheltered in deep dug-outs and in cellars beneath collapsed buildings though they had inflicted heavy casualties. The optimism noticeable in all quarters as to the effect of the bombardments was rapidly dispelled as the strength of the German

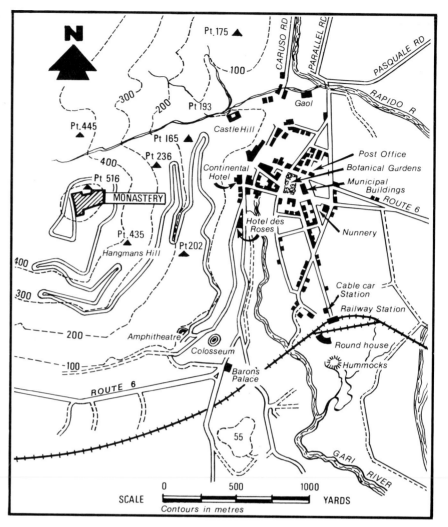

Above left: Map 6 The New Zealanders' attack on Cassino town, 15-24 March 1944.

Left: A New Zealand infantryman, armed with a Thompson sub-machine gun, advances among the ruins.
/*Alexander Turnbull Library, Wellington*

Above: Every house that is not completely destroyed may contain snipers and bombers, so it must be carefully searched./*IWM*

Right: A New Zealand platoon HQ is established in a ruined building./*IWM*

resistance became apparent. By 1250 hours A Company's leading platoons had advanced 100yd to the nunnery and to the vicinity of the road junction 150yd east of it, protected by the barrage and a thick smokescreen which covered the town, and in very difficult conditions were pressing forward. Cassino was in a state of utter destruction, every building in complete ruins and open spaces and former roadways churned up or covered in debris and badly cratered. Some streets could hardly be found, much less used. The men had a most unenviable task, scrambling over rubble, through mud and bomb craters half-full of water, and exposed to incessant rifle and machine gun fire. A little after 1300 hours communications between forward companies and Battalion HQ were broken and the companies lost touch with each other in the confused jumble of the ruins.

'One of B Company's tasks on the way to their objective was to clear the lower slopes of Castle Hill to prepare for D Company's attack on the Castle. Fire at close range from German posts there, however, forced the company to swing to the left towards the middle of the town, some of the men going over as far as the nunnery. By 1400 hours the company had been unable to get farther forward than the line of the nunnery, but an hour later was again moving forward, being finally held up for the day with its forward platoon at a school about 350yd short of the Continental Hotel. Sgt T. W. Tulloch, a platoon sergeant in B Company, took command, when his platoon commander was wounded, though he himself was wounded by grenade splinters. Getting in touch with the nearest tank he arranged for its support and overcame the nearest enemy strongpoint. His strength had then been reduced to 12 men and he was beyond the limit of further tank support, but with his platoon weapons alone he assaulted the next strongpoint about 75yd away; this was a group of strongly fortified houses at the base of Castle Hill. He and his platoon were driven back, but he then established his men in a strong position on the flank and partly neutralised the strongpoint. Until ordered by his company commander to report to the RAP, where he was evacuated, he stayed with his men; throughout the fighting his aggressive tactics and his personal example were excellent. He was awarded the Distinguished Conduct Medal, commonly regarded as the equivalent for other ranks as the Distinguished Service Order. . . . Meanwhile, the supporting tanks, 7 Troop on the right and 8 Troop on the left, had been delayed by craters on the roads before entering Cassino. At about 1330 hours 7 Troop succeeded in reaching the southern end of Caruso road, 100yd south-west of the gaol, but the destruction of buildings and streets

had created such appalling obstacles that the troop could get no further than the Continental Hotel, 600yd farther south. From the position it had reached, however, 7 Troop, which was under fire from the slopes of Castle Hill, vigorously engaged enemy posts. On the other flank 8 Troop made its way slowly over piles of rubble and round craters past the gaol and the nunnery, and shortly after 1400 hours, reached the road junction east of the latter which A Company had passed an hour or more earlier. The troop continued to move slowly forward though sometimes, to find a route, it was necessary to make a reconnaissance on foot and on occasions the men had to clear a path with picks and shovels. According to one personal account, "the confusion was such when the town was entered that our own tanks did not know which buildings we had occupied and at times we came under fire from them with armour-piercing shells."

'From 1730 to 1800 hours the artillery again fired on the final barrage line and after that concentrated on the railway station area, from which enemy mortars had been troublesome. However, the expectation that the leading companies would then be able to reach the objective was not realised. The scene at dusk was described by Lt Milne, commanding C Company: "Consolidate was the order at dusk. In the maze positions were sought out, with men milling about, stretcher bearers getting out the wounded, and shells falling all over the place. No supplies could be brought in but luckily each tank had carried ammunition, even primed grenades, so there was no shortage." To add to the desolation and to the discomfort of the tired, disillusioned and disappointed troops, rain began

Above: Collecting wounded under a Red Cross flag. This was not always possible and there were a number of unfortunate incidents during the attack when stretcher bearers were killed by the enemy, despite such obvious markings./*IWM*

Above: German paratroopers, captured by the New Zealanders stand under guard, near a Sherman tank./IWM

to fall just after dusk and continued heavily throughout the night. With the moon obscured it was pitch dark; movement was almost impossible. The water-filled craters made conditions hopeless and night operations simply sould not be planned or carried out. No hot food could be taken up and the men, saturated and chilled, passed a miserable night.'

Fortunately it was not all gloom, for D Company's operations against Castle Hill had gone much better. In the early part of the afternoon they had been held up outside Cassino by the slow advance of A and B Companies in the town, but eventually they got going. Here follows an eyewitness account of part of the fighting as the attack developed. At about 1300 hours, 16 Platoon was at the foot of an almost sheer cliff below Point 165 and began a very difficult and slow climb. Pte McNiece, a Bren gunner in No 1 Section described the events thus:

'It was about 1300 hours when we reached the foot of Castle Hill and started to scramble up the cliff face where a goat would have had difficulty getting up. After a very hot and hard climb we reached the shelter of a very large rock, about 100ft from the top of the hill. Cpl McInnes, i/c No 1 Section, directed myself (Bren gunner) and Bill Stockwell (2 i/c Bren) to go out to the right and protect the platoon's right flank. We hadn't advanced 10yd when I looked back and saw Cpl McInnes with two Jerries with their hands in the air; they were scouts posted on the lookout to warn their HQ of our approach but we were so close on the artillery barrage and the Jerries were as deep down as possible in their dugout, so that they failed to hear us or see us.

If they had spotted us we would never have had a chance to climb the hill face; from their position they could have quite easily picked us all off. As Bill and I came to the edge of the rock I noticed a concrete pillbox on the top of the hill – it was about 12ft square with a small window two feet square and four feet from the ground. I said to Bill: "That's a likely place for a Jerry or two; what about having a look" . . . I raised the Bren to my hip and made for the pillbox which was about 20yd distant. When I had covered the distance I heard Bill yell: "Look out for the Spandau" and he fired past me into the window. I did not see the Spandau but made a dash for the side of the pillbox. Bill kept on firing and the Jerry withdrew the Spandau. I was now between the window and the corner of the pillbox, a distance of five feet. My first thoughts were of the three 36 HE grenades that I had on me and in a few seconds I had pulled the pin out and slipped one grenade through the window. There was a lovely explosion, dust and splinters of stone and wood come flying out of the window; a few seconds later there was a clatter at my feet and there lay a Jerry stick grenade smoking and spitting out sparks – without stopping to think I grabbed it up and flung it over the cliff – I didn't hear it go off but the boys in the rear of the platoon said it went off just below them! I immediately slipped another grenade through the window and it went off with a bang; another stick grenade came through the window and landed just out of my reach – I fell flat on my face and hoped for the best; the seconds seemed like ages; then there was a terrific explosion. Dirt and rocks flew in all directions I was completely obscured in the dust and Bill said to himself "Mac's had it". My head felt as if it had been bashed in and my ears rang and ached cruelly. [He was evacuated to hospital on 8 April suffering from ruptured ear drums. *Author*] When the dust cleared away I was standing by the window with the Bren gun held out at arm's length pouring a stream of hot lead through the window. I then threw my last HE 36 grenade inside and stood with my back to the wall wondering what to do next.

'All the time this was happening a Spandau was firing past a corner of the pillbox and the hot lead was only missing my legs by inches. I looked down at Bill and saw him calling the Jerries to come out. I then looked at the window and saw a Red Cross flag held out. I called on Jerry to "Kamarad" and he replied "No, no, wounded". I looked through the window and saw some wounded Jerries lying on the floor. I called Bill up and covered him while he entered, then I scrambled in and covered the Jerries while Bill took their arms away. At the far end of the pillbox there was a ladder down into a huge dugout about 12ft square and 15ft deep. Jerries were filing up the ladder with their hands in the air. When we counted them up there were two dead, 23 alive, five of whom were wounded. The pillbox was a German Company HQ of the Paras. The captain, a 21-year old boy, was dead and the 2 i/c, a lieutenant, was seriously wounded. After we had disarmed them I sent them one at a time, down the hill to our officer – all this was done in a few minutes. In the meantime the Jerries in the Castle had come into action – mortars, rifle grenades, and bullets were flying in all directions. Capt McInnes had stopped a burst of Spandau in the back and was dead. Gerry Marsh, a boy of 21, was also killed by a Spandau and several others wounded. . . .'

Both McNiece and Stockwell were awarded well deserved Military Medals for their bravery in this action. By nightfall, Castle Hill and Point 165 had been successfully occupied by D Company, although a number of enemy strongpoints were still holding out and giving much trouble.

The night of the 15/16 March was to be a momentous one for the troops of 5 Indian Brigade, who relieved the 25th NZ Battalion on Castle Hill and their epic capture of Hangman's Hill would be the next bloody chapter in the Cassino story.

Ayo Gurkhali!
'Epic of Monastery Hill – in a circle of death, they fought on. Nine day wonder of Monastery Hill, above Cassino – a wonder of grim heroism in conditions of maddening thirst and near famine . . .'

That is how the British press headlined the battle of Hangman's Hill. The newsreports went on:
' . . . They clawed their way up the hill's rugged slopes on 15 March, only to find themselves cut off on its eastern slope. Now they are back with Allied troops, having made their way through German lines. One company, led by Lt Michael Drinkall, of London, led the attack on that rain-drenched night . . . They crept through Cassino and up the slope to Hangman's Hill, jutting out of the face of the mountain. Units following up Drinkall's company were ambushed in the town. They were not able to reach him till the morning of March 17 when the Germans were counter-attacking and blasting Drinkall's men from their foxholes. Reinforcements led by Lt

Below: Col West, CO 1/6 Rajputanas and his company officers climbing Monastery Hill during a recce prior to the attack./*MOD New Delhi*

Angus Samuels of Salisbury, Rhodesia, came up at the critical moment. Samuels seized a Bren gun and sprayed the Germans, while the Gurkhas closed in with their long knives. The Germans kept their distance from then on though they constantly shelled the hillside. Lt Jack Miles of London and Lt Norman Costello of Carlisle, commanded other reinforcement companies. They sent patrols to within 550yd of the Abbey. Capt Fred Anakin of Liverpool directed the dropping of supplies for the air to the marooned men, who had no food for 36 hours . . . the original party had their canteens only half filled with water because they had to cut down the weight of their equipment to a minimum. The only food they carried were biscuits. Then a party of porters got through, in spite of heavy losses, with two biscuits and half a sardine per man. The men suffered terribly from thirst. Water patrols were sent out all along the enemy held mountain. They found a bomb crater which held a few gallons of water and drained it inspite of German snipers and mortar fire . . . "We drank that down to a reasonable level, and then found a dead mule in the bottom", the survivors reported, "after that everyone went thirsty for five days in a row, except for small quantities dropped by American planes." The supplies, dropped by parachute and in the papier-mache belly tanks, allowed only one third of a tin of rations a day for each man. The troops watched helplessly as many packets and parachutes drifted over the German lines. Their one contact with the outside world was a radio worked at brief intervals in order to save batteries by Capt Gerald Evans of Edinburgh. 'We used to like to listen to the BBC news about us," said the men.'

Top: *Ayo Gurkhali!* **Men of a Gurkha battalion move up a mountain road towards Cassino.**/*IWM*

Above: Fresh chapatis are packed into containers for air dropping to the beleagured Gurkhas on Hangman's Hill – but very few ever arrived. /*MOD New Delhi*

Right: In full view of the enemy, the Gurkhas on Hangman's Hill collect air dropped supplies under heavy fire./*MOD New Delhi*

A newspaper reporter can perhaps be excused for using a little artist's licence to bolster up a poor story, but in the case of the Hangman's Hill operation there was no need to embroider the truth. The regimental history of the 9th Gurkha Rifles tells the story in a more matter-of-fact, but equally exciting way:

'With the capture of Castle Hill the way was opened to advance across the slopes of Monte Cassino. At dusk 1/4 Essex relieved the New Zealanders in the ruins of the Castle and a company was despatched to test the enemy dispositions. First resistance was encountered at Point 165, the lowest hairpin bend of the road, which climbed to the Monastery in a series of switchbacks across the face of the mountain. The enemy strong-point was seized, creating room for manoeuvre. Whereupon 1/6 Rajputana Rifles and the First Battalion prepared to enter the battle . . . In conformity with the New Zealand belief in the likelihood of a breakthrough, an ambitious role had been entrusted to 5 Indian Brigade. Each battalion would seize a rung of the ladder up the mountainside which led to the embattled Monastery upon the crest. With the Essex providing a firm base at the Castle and its environs, 1/6 Rajputana Rifles would pass through to secure the hairpin bends of the switchback road which cut double niches across the face of the mountain toward a rocky outcrop immediately beneath the Monastery, at the point where the slopes of Monte Cassino curved westward into the Liri valley. This outcrop bore on its platform a shattered pylon formerly had carried an aerial ropeway. It was shown on military maps as Point 435, but to the soldiery it was Hangman's Hill.

'At 2000 hours, in dense darkness and under a thin soaking rain 1/6 Rajputana Rifles led the way down the Rapido valley. Around the foot of the mountain the adversaries bickered on. Intermittent harassing shoots swept all approaches. As the Rajputanas neared Cassino town they were caught by a vicious concentration. Part of the battalion managed to keep direction and to push through; the remainder scattered in the darkness and failed to re-assemble. The leading Rajputana companies reached the Castle, passed through the Essex at the lower hairpin bend and thrust in a gallant assault against the upper switchback. Success was denied them; this key feature, second only in importance to Hangman's Hill, remained in enemy hands.

'At 1900 hours First Battalion moved from Monte Castellone to the Brigade area below Cairo village . . . At midnight the Battalion continued down the Rapido valley. The narrow trail was crowded with men and mule trains moving in the opposite direction. It was raining heavily and cohesive movements were difficult. "We could only force our way through" wrote Col Nangle (CO of 1/9th

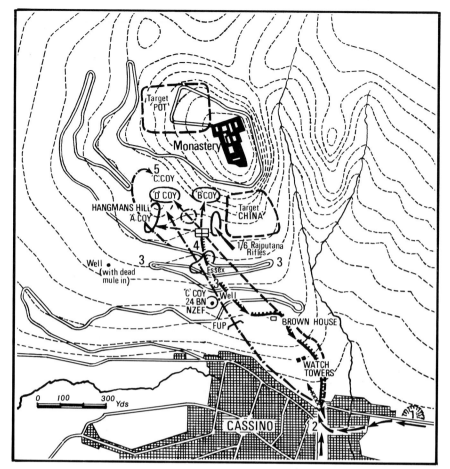

Above: Map 7 Action on Hangman's Hill, 15-25 March 1944.

Gurkha Rifles), "by pushing and shoving; as a consequence we were wet and exasperated when we reached the quarry at the outskirts of Cassino." Here Col West of the Rajputanas was encountered anxiously waiting news of his companies, which had embarked on their missions on the mountainside ahead. In lieu of tidings Col Nangle deemed it essential to push on. He led his men forward across the rubble and broken masonry which marked the edge of Cassino town. In single file the Gurkhas mounted a sort of walled valley which led to the lower slopes. When they gained the hillside they discovered two exits – one to the west along the contours of the mountain and the other which promised to reach the open ground above the town. C Company continued through the western exit and D Company turned upwards.

'As the latter company groped forward, Spandau fire opened at close range, followed by showers of grenades from nearby ruins. Fifteen men were struck down in five minutes. Attempts to bypass the enemy failed; there seemed to be snipers and bombers everywhere. The night was growing thin and Col Nangle was faced with the possibility of first light finding his three companies strung out in single file. He therefore deployed his men and endeavoured to press clear of the shattered streets and to gain his start line on the lower hillside. Before this could be accomplished the morning broke, with enemies ensconced on all sides. When Brig Bateman examined 5 Brigade's dispositions he found the sweep across the hillside to be at a standstill. The lower hairpin bend, little more than an outwork of the Castle position, was all that could be shown for the first night's fighting. Of three battalions only five companies had managed to reach the battlefield. Beset with pressing problems it seems unlikely that he gave more than a thought to C Company of the 9th Gurkhas, which had disappeared, leaving no trace.

'In early afternoon Corps artillery, in planning its fire programmes, asked if it would be safe to shoot on Hangman's Hill. New Zealand observers from beyond the Rapido reported that they had detected movement around the outcrop. At 1400 hours a radio telephonist of A Company grew tense; faint signals were coming through. Within a few minutes Battalion, Brigade, Division and Corps had received the electrifying news that C Company had traversed the hillside, had seized Hangman's Hill and had consolidated it against opposition. High on the shoulder of the mountain with enemies on all sides, an audacious success had repaired all the failures elsewhere. These tidings changed the course of the battle. All resources of 4 Indian Division were immediately diverted to the support of Capt Drinkall and his men. At 1600 hours Col Nangle called an officers' conference. That night the remainder of the Battalion would fight its way through to Hangman's Hill; each section, platoon and company would be despatched without recall.'

The hair-raising climb made by 9th Gurkhas that night led by their commanding officer along the goat path, no more than a foot wide, on the sheer face of the ravine, is an epic story in itself, but unfortunately there is not room to tell it here in detail. As the press report stated, Capt Samuels of D Company rushed up the remaining slopes at the head of his men and arrived in the nick of time to prevent a German counter-attack from crushing the right flank of the position: '... Snatching a Bren gun from a dead Gurkha, Capt Samuels raked the assault groups as they appeared over the crown of a low ridge a few yards away. His swift and gallant action turned the tide.' D Company spread its platoons along the crest of the platform, to reinforce C Company's thin line. A Company extended the position on the left flank and B Company did likewise on the right. Battalion HQ was established in a small wadi below the road in the rear of B Company. Thus began the ordeal which as their history relates: 'made the 9th Gurkhas the best-known battalion in Italy. Clinging like limpets to their shaggy boss in the shadow of the monastery walls, encircled by tenacious

enemies, they impelled the battle for Cassino to take shape around them.'

Lt Jack Miles was one of those indomitable fighters on Hangman's Hill. Here is how he remembers the more mundane problems of their long siege:

'Cassino was my first action as an infantryman. Having served from 1939 in other branches, I arrived in January 1944, to a scenario which to my mind, came straight from a typical Hollywood war movie. For Cassino seemed to have everything that the most exaggerated war film should contain – a "Mad Mile" which made every daylight approach to the town a gamble with the German shells; a battered Monastery overlooking our every movement; near starvation for those of us who were cut off for nine days; chivalry at times on both sides; and – for those of us fortunate enough to survive – a happy ending.

'The March battle was the first proof that I had of the indisputable fact that the chap who knows least about the overall course of events is the one who is actually doing the fighting. I have certainly learned far more about the March battle for Cassino by reading about it, than I did by participating in it. So my memories of events, to be original, must of neccessity be parochial, personal and probably petty in the overall picture. With the exception of C Company, the 1/9th Gurkha Rifles were forced to "hole up" in the rubble of Cassino town for the night of 15/16 March, before moving on towards Hangman's Hill during the night 16/17 March.

'It was during that enforced delay that Maj Paddy Radcliffe, B Company commander went missing. I was with him in B Company HQ when he left to traverse no more than 50yd of ruined streets and buldings for a COs conference in Battalion HQ. He never arrived. Nobody saw him fall, nobody heard anything to indicate what had happened and his disappearance was one of the mysteries of the war to my mind.* It led to my taking command of B Company. A sobering responsibility just six months after being commissioned, although that did not occur to me at the time. Certainly I was thankful for the experience and support forthcoming from the Subedar and Jemadar† who still survived when I took over. Unfortunately both were wounded soon after – the Jemadar by one of our own smoke shells, a splinter from which smashed my spectacles as I stood alongside him.

* It was later presumed that he had been killed by a sniper.

† Subedar=Captain; Jemadar=Lieutenant, both were Viceroy's Commissioned Officers.

Above: Indian troops of 8 Indian Division set out on patrol in the snow. The Division served with both Fifth and Eighth Armies in Italy, winning four VCs, including Kamal Ram of the 8th Punjab Regiment, who, at 19, was the war's youngest VC.
/MOD New Delhi

'Food soon became an obsession – we were virtually surrounded and supplies were extremely scarce. I shall never know who decided that American K Rations would make a suitable diet for Gurkha troops – but, on the rare occasions that airdrops were successful, that is what we got! The contents included small tins of self heating soups, various processed meat products and other odd items which seemed more suitable to a school picnic than to the battlefield. Despite their hunger, the Gurkhas would not risk breaking their Hindu faith and its laws by eating anything produced from the cow. So, when we shared out the contents of a K ration packet, they would bring me a tin of meat product and ask me to identify it from the label before they would eat it. I must admit that I told the occasional white lie. After all, one K ration was intended as one meal for one man. We had, at best one K ration for one man for one day, at worst, one between three men for one day. Oh yes! It also included that great American invention chewing gum. Here I scored – it was not overpopular with the Gurkhas, so I gradually accumulated a huge blob of gum which I stuck on the side of my sangar until I felt hungry again. Water was a problem too. The position occupied by B Company was some 380-400yd below the Monastery on a steep, rocky slope from which every trace of vegetation had been blasted, and where no pools had formed. We relied on what was sent up to us from Battalion HQ and soon learned to let the water settle, and to leave the last drop – this was invariably muddy. It was not until after the action that I learned that our supplies were dredged from bomb craters and shell holes. A rumour also circulated later claiming that one of our watering points was found to contain a dead mule after it had been used – I prefer to discount that story!

'Our planes faced an almost impossible task of trying to drop supply containers into a very restricted area, on the side of a steep hill and in face of enemy fire. So very few of these containers fell anywhere near our positions. Those that did were recovered by my chaps in B Company under extremely dangerous conditions, perhaps involving a 200-yard dash across, or down, the rocky hillside, under sniper fire, with a slow climb back to Company HQ with a heavy load. Imagine the heartbreak when hungry men unpacked those containers to find ammunition, or wireless batteries. Not once did a food container fall in B Company's area. Of course we got our share from the containers which dropped within the total battalion area. An additional benefit from the containers was the protection afforded by the heavy felt lined canvas used to wrap the drop. March on a rocky Italian mountainside does not exactly provide ideal camping conditions – we had no overcoats or blankets, so the "bedding from heaven" was most usful.

'The withdrawal from Hangman's Hill was nothing short of a modern miracle. I led B Company off the hill with Col Nangle ahead of me, feeling his way through the darkness between a barrage of fire from our own guns laid down to protect us. Col Nangle did a magnificent job that night – we literally came out in single file, through the enemy lines and to my knowledge not a man was lost. Even the Gurkha who fell asleep on the slopes of Castle Hill, during a halt in the withdrawl was recovered safely at first light by the Royal West Kents. My first thoughts on reaching B Echelon centered on food and bed. After a huge meal, I rolled between blankets and was wide awake after two hours! Not surprising perhaps, after nine days with so little sleep and so much noise of battle continuing for 24 hours each day every day. Thirty years later – in 1974 – I returned to an unrecognisable Cassino, apart from the monastery. The hillside which had been shorn of all vegetation by bomb and shell, was now a mass of trees, gorse and shrubs. I'll swear the hill was now twice as high and three times as steep as it seemed in 1944, but perhaps that was due to Anno Domini. However, it served to bring home to me the events on the nine days of my life which I doubt I will ever forget. In the war cemetery later on, on that sunny day in 1974, I realised even more how fortunate I was to be standing there looking up at the memorial to the 190 or so comrades in the battalion who fell during the Cassino campaign.'

And on the crest of that shaggy outcrop known as Hangman's Hill, a giant boulder bears the badge of the 9th Gurkhas whose epic story will be told and retold as long as memory remains.

Anzio—Hell's Half Acre

'The silence of the mist shrouded morning was misleading. It gave no warning of the hell that was to be Anzio. The lonely stretch of Italian coast looked gaunt and uninviting to the first Thunderbirdmen who hit the beach on the heels of the 3rd – the Marne Division.'

So begins the account of 45th Infantry Division's involvement in the battle of the Anzio beachhead which was to develop into one of the most bitter, sustained and hard fought battles Fifth Army experienced in Italy. It has been described as a soldier's battle, fought against a well organised, brave and stubborn enemy, and it created much camaraderie between American and British servicemen as some of the pictures show. Here is how a staff writer in *Yank* described Anzio in that popular soldiers' newspaper:

'Crammed with TNT, blood and fighting men and women, this Allied colony has become one of the hottest spots on earth. It measures only some 14 miles in length by about seven in depth, but its 90-odd square miles of flat and fertile farmlands have taken some of this war's greatest concentrations of fire and assault. Every square inch of it is vulnerable to enemy fire. A ring of Kraut-held hills looks down on the fighting line and on these twin resort towns.* German observers hidden on these heights place shells in the harbour, in the streets, and can place one in the living room of any residence you name. Kraut dive-bombers sneak through the air screen and lay their eggs on town and country. The German High Command seeing in the beachhead the only last-straw victory to hand its suffering public, has hit the area with everything it can spare from the main Italian front, but the Fifth Army men have held every time. The High Command has even unleashed two of the Wehrmacht's choicer secret weapons: one a radio-controlled bomb which our ack-ack gunners have brought down; the other a remote-controlled tank – already dubbed the Doodlebug – carrying 130 pounds of explosives, which gunners have also knocked out. Soon after the bulletless landing on 22 January the Germans formed up and began their all out attempts to push the little beachhead into the sea. They hit it with wave after wave of tank supported infantry, which one man said: "came at us like packs of wolves". Air attacks by the full weight of the MAAF,* however, aided the ground forces in repulsing those assaults. From the beginning the fighting see-sawed back and forth so much that strange situations resulted. A German medical unit, surrounded by an American outfit, was allowed to pick up its casualties and go back into its own lines. One strategic cross-roads called *Femina Morta* (Dead Woman) had Germans in farm houses on one side of the road and GIs in houses on the other side.

'Many people have lost count of the number of times the "Factory Building" near Carroceto, scene of the heaviest fighting, has changed hands; a modern American "Lost Battalion" came back after standing against the enemy for nine days, during three of which it was surrounded. Rear areas receive almost as much fire as the front lines. Early in the operation a hospital was bombed, killing 23, including two nurses, six patients, and one Red Cross worker, and wounding 68; later German long range artillery shells screamed into the hospital area, killing two more nurses and wounding seven officers and men. A field bakery well toward the rear is still turning out 13,000 loaves a day, despite a all-day shelling of its vicinity. Already two of the bakers are wearing Purple Hearts.† Shells have hit quartermaster dumps, spraying meat and vegetable hash, and one well aimed 88 even struck a newly landed pile of cigarettes. The few civilians left have moved into caverns and catacombs beneath the beachhead towns, venturing out only to sell what wine remains. At least one baby has been born since the landing, a girl, delivered a mile from the front line by a country doctor who did the job with 16 candles and a flashlight.

'Now, with the beachhead nearly two months old, its defenders are faced with a semi-circle of 10 German divisions – crack divisions from Northern Italy and at least one from Southern France. With German forces

* The writer was of course referring to Anzio and Nettuno – hardly 'resort towns' during the beachhead battle!

* MAAF – Mediterranean Allied Air Forces.

† The Purple Heart was awarded to an American soldier who was wounded in action.

in Italy believed to total between 18 and 20 divisions, the beachhead can realise the importance it has assumed. It has drawn off half of von Kesselring's forces. The chips are down; the hand is being played.'

In order to describe the 'Hell that was Anzio' I have chosen graphic accounts of the fighting as experienced by American GIs of 45 Infantry Division in the area known as 'The Caves', and by British Tommies of 1 Infantry Division in 'The Wadis/Gullies', both of which must have been very similar to the appalling conditions suffered by soldiers in the trenches of World War I. The war history of the 'Thunderbirds' reads:
'On the moonlight night of 15 February, the 2nd Battalion moved into position on the north-south highway, three kilometres in front of the huge railroad overpass. The Battalion that night relieved British and American units, taking over their foxholes, slit-trenches, and dugouts. Company E on the right, Company G on the left, Company F between, Company H in reserve. Ahead of the battalion stretched miles of flat, open terrain, broken only by ditches barely deep enough to conceal a crawling soldier. Houses, occupied by enemy troops, and sparse wooded areas cast sharp outlines against the sky. To the right was Aprilia, the so-called factory, where another unit (the 179th Infantry) had met bitter resistance a few days before, suffering heavy losses. Behind the front line companies, in a labyrinth of man made caves, was the Battalion Command Post. The caves had been dug into a shale ridge and extended underground in all directions for thousands of yards. Almost impervious to enemy shellfire, the caves became headquarters for the staff, the medical aid men, and the field artillery radio crew. Trucks could drive within the tunnels, so the caves became a supply point as well. In the action that followed they became the battalion's last point of defence.

'Tired from their night march and the constant stop and go that marks a frontline relief, the men settled into their shallow slit-trenches and relaxed as best they could. Dawn was approaching. There was silence for a while and then suddenly from far away came the whine of approaching shells, then the screams, rumble and crash as the projectiles hit. The men huddled in their holes and waited tensely as the shelling increased. Over the noise of the explosions came the distant sound of enemy guns. Shells blew men out of their shallow trenches. The cry of the wounded – "Medics, medics" – pierced the air. To the cramped, nervous men crouching to the ground, the barrage seemed endless, but suddenly the shelling ceased. Across the rocky flat from Aprilla rolled German light tanks and behind them charging infantrymen.

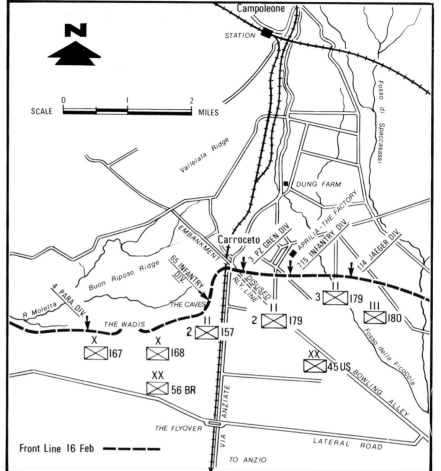

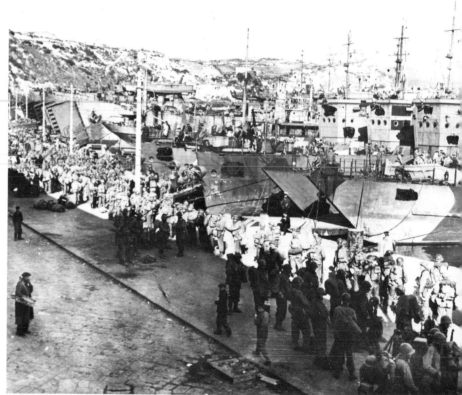

The full brunt of the enemy assault* struck Company E head on. Riflemen and machine gunners cut down the German infantry, which had broken into the company area, to fight the battle alone. At 25yd range a TD (Tank Destroyer) opened fire on the enemy foot troops with .50 calibre machine guns and tommy guns, killing many of the attackers. To the TD crew went the credit for breaking up the first assault, but their ammunition was expended and they were forced to withdraw. All morning long the German infantry moved across the open fields, into our interlocking fire. Hundreds died, but the assault waves never ceased. Company G, on the left about the caves, was also under attack by German tanks and infantry. Artillery fire stopped the tanks, by the enemy pushed on, crawling through draws and ravines despite the shellfire from Company G. Some 200 enemy soldiers closed in on the right flank and died. On the left, German infantry overran one platoon in the wake of an artillery barrage. 1-Lt Joe Robertson, the company commander, ordered friendly artillery fire down on his own positions. Though it brought casualties to Company G, it slaughtered the exposed enemy. Assaulting Germans plunged into foxholes to engage the men of the company in hand-to-hand combat. Under continued pres-

* This was the first phase of Operation Fisch Fang (Catching Fish) 16-19 February 1944.

Above left: Map 8 The Caves, front line 16-19 February 1944.

Left: The invasion force embarks. American GIs filing on board LCIs and LCTs at a harbour in the Naples area, prior to being transported to Anzio./*US Army*

Top: GIs dash ashore onto Anzio beaches from their landing craft./*US Army*

Above and right: Anzio. The landing was virtually unopposed as these scenes, photographed on X-Ray Beach, soon after dawn on 22 January show. White tape indicates the boundary of the path to which vehicles were confined by soft ground./*US Army*

sure, the hard hit and weakened platoon was forced to withdraw. The Germans held the ground.

'There was no longer any doubt that this was a determined effort to drive the Allied forces from the beachhead. The fury of the German assault was almost unbelievable. Prisoners and dead Germans from 16 different regiments were identified in the assault. Seven divisions were used, including Panzer and paratroops, fighting in the Campo di Carne – which, ironically enough, translated means "Field of Meat". In the afternoon the Panzers attacked again, assaulting the right platoon, overrunning the position and knocking out two anti-tank guns. With these guns knocked out, the tanks moved directly to the foxholes of the valiantly fighting riflemen. At point blank range, they fired on the men. Dazed from the constant explosions – defenceless against the tanks – many of the men were forced to surrender. At dark the first day, the attack slowed, but did not stop. There seemed to be a brief breathing spell for a renewed effort. Through the night the Germans slowly and methodically infiltrated into the disrupted positions of the front line, and engaged the handful of men who were holding the last hope of the defence. In the sectors of the 179th and 180th Infantry Regiments, the enemy artillery had concentrated artillery fire and patrol efforts to give the appearance of impending attack, in an attempt to appear even more powerful than they were. In the light of flares, the Luftwaffe scattered bombs on artillery batteries, supply and ammunition dumps, mortar and infantry positions. Communication lines were broken by artillery fire, and it was necessary to rely on radio messages for contact between the units and their commanders.

62

Far left: Amphibious trucks bring supplies ashore at Anzio./US Army

Left: Ready to come ashore at Anzio. A Landing Ship Tank unloads Fifth Army troops into a Higgins boat to take them ashore./US Army

Centre left: German soldiers clean their weapons near Nettuno as they wait for another attack, 31 March 1944. /IWM

Bottom left: American and British troops captured in the Nettuno bridgehead area, being marched through Rome, February 1944./IWM

Top: A good shot of a German SP gun – the 15cm heavy infantry howitzer, seen here in a firing position between the ruins of Carroceto near Aprilia. In the background is a Sd Kfz 251 halftrack and a knocked out Sherman tank, 26 February 1944./IWM

Above: Drying their feet at Nettuno. Two GIs take time out to dry their feet and change their socks after wading ashore from a landing craft, during the unopposed landing. /US Army

Left: GIs on patrol make their way through a path marked by white tape by the engineers which has been cleared of mines and booby traps./US Army

'Under cover of darkness patrols began extensive operations. The Germans brought in supplies and more troops to reinforce their drive. It was obvious that they were cheered by their initial assault, and would spare neither men nor material until the Anzio beachhead no longer existed. Shortly after midnight the enemy began to move forward again. The new attack began from the vicinity of the railway overpass. German infantry infiltrated in groups of 20 and 30, while the artillery fires of both sides continued throughout the night. Thirteen additional enemy tanks began operating along the main highway. In the effort to stop the German onslaught, the concentrated fires of the beachhead artillery was used many times near the division's lines. Requests were radioed for air support from every available air unit. Shortly after dawn on 17 February several squadrons of heavy bombers flew over Anzio to bomb enemy areas. This began the succession of flights which continued for several days; involving the entire Mediterranean Allied Air Force in the strongest support ever given to ground forces. Such stubborn resistance was not maintained without considerable losses in equipment and personnel; there were few, if any, replacements for those who became casualties, and the men who remained were forced to exert every effort to fill the gap left by the fallen. With only 18 men of Company E left, Capt Sparks began a withdrawal at daylight of 17 February. The Germans continued their offensive, this time with the full force striking Company G. The crossfire forced them to stop, leaving scattered groups of dead and wounded lying in the ravine. At one point an odd shaped X formed by dead Germans showed where machine gunners had laid down their fire. Contact patrols sent out battled their way through infiltrating Germans. Finding no friendly troops, they fought their way back to the Battalion sector.

'All day enemy soldiers, tanks and self-propelled weapons advanced towards the overpass. The Germans pressed every advantage. Enemy artillery poured into the Battalion sector without let-up, and German foot troops appeared on all sides. Battalion medics moved about the area, carrying seriously wounded men into the aid station in the caves, where they were drugged to relieve their pain. Water was needed, but only occasionally could carriers work their way forward to the caves. In a nearby draw trickled a stream in which lay corpses of enemy dead. The water ran blood red, but many men filled their canteens, boiled it and drank.

'At dusk on 18 February, Sgt Garcia crawled through a draw to the Battalion CP and warned the commander that a company of

64

Left: American soldiers enjoy a hot meal in a dining room outside an evacuation hospital in the Anzio beachhead area. Note the sandbag parapet to provide some protection against shelling and bombing./US Army

Centre left: Jane of the *Daily Mirror* provides a novel anti-malaria warning in the beachhead./IWM

Bottom left: A carrier platoon awaits the order to move more ammunition forward during the Allied attack in the Anzio area./IWM

Right: An Anzio padre leaves his 'rectory' in the wadis. /IWM

Below: 'Housing' in the dykework along the Mussolini Canal, occupied by men of 1SSF./Col R. D. Burhans

Below centre: 'Braves' of 1SSF man a 57mm anti-tank gun in the Anzio area. /Col R. D. Burhans

Bottom: German POWs captured by 1SSF in the Anzio area awaiting interrogation./Col R. D. Burhans

enemy was coming close. Infiltrating Germans were everywhere, moving singly or in pairs. The tunnels became a defensive position. Every man fired into the surrounding forces. Riflemen lobbed hand grenades over the bluff into the midst of the advancing enemy. Inside the caves, Capt Hubbert, artillery liaison officer, radioed back for fire on the battalion position and the caves. For two hours Allied artillery swept the draws and ditches.

'As the Germans struck again with fresh troops, the weary men in the caves continued to hold on. They were outnumbered and outflanked, always low on ammunition and always under shelling, but now they fought with hope. Front line rumour had said that the British were trying to relieve them. After dark, a battalion of British infantry began its march into the sector. The men listened to the offbeat drone of enemy bombers and the sputter of the "butterfly" bombs and wondered if they would make it. An hour later, as the firefights broke out, the new battalion made its arrival known. They had fought their way in foot by foot, they had been bombed, they had suffered heavy casulties, they had lost their heavy weapons and ammunition, but they were there. The men in the caves welcomed them with heart-felt joy. Because the British had lost so many heavy weapons, most of the division's machine gun and mortar crews remained in action. Throughout the day the Germans continued to attack from the rear, closing in upon the British. The crowded sector was a maelstrom of activity. The exhausted troops inside the caves awaiting orders to move out were fully aware that they would have to fight their way back into friendly lines, but they were eager to go. The battalion had plotted the withdrawal over the route of supply, but the Germans kept a tenacious grip upon that ground. A reserve platoon was brought up, and they

65

attacked to secure ground from which they might be able to cover the withdrawal with their fire. Also, they would attempt to establish contact with the British to secure, as much as possible, the 2nd Battalion's avenue of escape.'

Unfortunately space does not allow me to include the whole of the enthralling story of the battalion's journey to the relative safety of rear of the beachhead area. However, there was bitter fighting all the way. Of the 2nd Battalion which entered the caves and slit trenches eight days before, less than one quarter returned. That was what it was like in the 'Caves' and life in the 'Wadis/Gullies' was no picnic either as the Official History of the Irish Guards relates:

'For three days and four nights the depleted battalion held the gullies against continual attack. It was a savage brutish troglodyte existence, in which there could be no sleep for anyone and no rest for any commander. The weather was almost the worst enemy, and the same torrential rain, which sent an icy flood swirling around our knees as we lurked in the gullies, would at times sweep away the earth that covered the poor torn bodies of casualties hastily buried in "The Boot". Wallowing in a network of gullies, isolated by day and errati-cally supplied by night, soaked to the skin, stupified by exhaustion and bombardment, surrounded by new and old corpses and yet patiently cheerful, the Guardsman dug trenches and manned them till they were blown in and then dug new ones, beat off attacks, changed positions, launched local attacks, stalked snipers, broke up patrols, evacuated the wounded, buried the dead and carried supplies. The bringing up of supplies every night was a recurrent nightmare. Carrying parties got lost, jeeps got bogged and as the swearing troops heaved at them, down came the shells. "What I remember most," said one officer, "is the long strain of hanging on all day to hear the list of casualties every evening, to see stretcher-bearers livid with fatigue, staggering past with their load, a dirty Red Cross flag held aloft as a precarious appeal." The life was one of unremitting drudgery. As Gibbon says of the Roman legions, active valour may often be present in nature, but such patient diligence can only be the fruit of habit and diligence. Every single man did his duty and more than his duty.'*

* History of the Irish Guards in the Second World War; by Major D.U.L. Fitzgerald.

Below: A 155mm 'Long Tom' blasting away in the Nettuno area./US Army

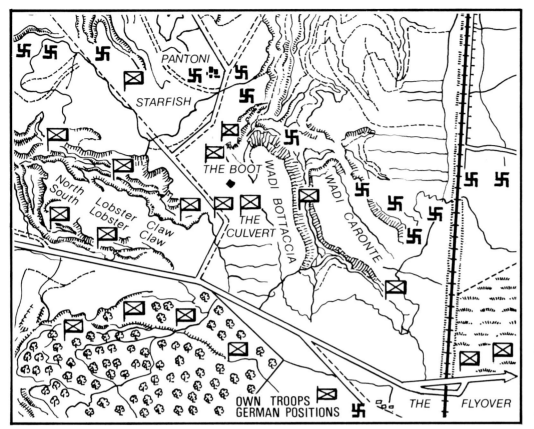

Left: Map 9 The Wadis, February-May 1944.

Below: The photo shows part of the area known as the 'wadis', which was very reminiscent of World War I trench warfare with all the similar horrors and discomforts./*IWM*

On the night of 24 February 1944, the 1st Battalion, The Duke of Wellington's Regiment, relieved the Irish Guards. This is how the relief was recorded in the CO's diary:

'In the evening the Battalion set out. With a rather defiant gaiety the troops climbed into the troop carrying lorries. I got into my carrier with John Streatfield. It was, as usual, full of the 22-set and its attendants. Going past Brigade HQ I saw the Brigadier standing by the road. He wished me luck. I felt that we needed it. Dusk was drawing in as we drove into the woods and bumped along the mud and potholes which were the twin components of the improvised road forming the channel of communications. About two miles from the Flyover we debussed. The Germans selected that moment for a bout of harassing fire in the woods, and the inevitable confusion of debussing in the dark was complicated by a number of casualties. As the shelling died down the companies were formed up and began to march to the rendezvous where the guides from Brigade HQ would meet us. Still in my carrier John and I pushed on. It was pitch dark. Reliefs were always an edgy business, both for the relieved and relieving units. The companies were late at the RV and, heavily loaded by the 22-set, Battalion HQ was even later.

'The track now rapidly deteriorated and soon became a mere mud-bath. The rather pampered personnel of Battalion HQ groaned under the weight of their loads as we floun-

dered along in the slimy black clay. The Germans began to shell heavily the Campo di Carne road. We had to cross this to get to the wadis and the ever-haunting fear, on relief nights loomed large. Would the troops be caught in the open? It was difficult to judge amongst the trees the exact position of the shelling, and I sent a message through to the leading companies to halt. Pushing up the track to the fringe of the wood it was possible to see that the fire was coming down further to our left, just on the line of the road. It was a terrifying sight and it made a lot of noise. The Boche knew a relief was being carried out somewhere in our sector that night and his artillery was diabolically active. At any moment it might shift to our area. There was no option but to plug on.

'We gained the road and at last could walk without lifting about a hundredweight of mud on each foot. It was pitch dark, but to our left the vista was balefully illuminated by the heavy defensive fire being brought down by the Boche on the road about 500yd away. We advanced down the road for about 200yd toward the barrage; here a track bore off to the right and to the culvert where Andrew Scott, the CO of the Irish Guards had his HQ. There we turned off the road and plugged on up the track. It was dotted with shell holes. At regular intervals along the first 100yd were the derelict carriers of the Irish Guards, all knocked out while trying to bring up rations the night before. As we passed the last I heard an ominous whistle and, with John, dived into a small ditch beside the track. The mortar shell burst on the track about 100yd away. "It's about 500yd still to go sir," said the Guardsman unemotionally. He had remained in a perpendicular position and, feeling rather abashed, I climbed up and joined him on the track. It seemed an age, but at last we reached a small bridge over a little gulley, which formed a culvert. This was our RV.

'The leading companies were already filing off to the right across country to take over positions there. I climbed down the bank into the little gulley, and edged past a wrecked jeep trailer into the culvert. Here was the RAP, also Andrew's HQ. That imperturable officer, wrapped in a duffle coat, presented his usual robust and faintly Regency appearance. The little culvert was crammed. The MO was dealing with a couple of recently wounded Guardsmen, and the RAP occupied half the space; the rest contained the elements of the HQs of both battalions, Dukes' signallers taking over from the Guards and my own officers trying to contact their opposite numbers. Andrew and I sat on a stretcher propped up on empty ration boxes and discussed the situation. The position was fluid in the extreme and the whole area was cut up

Left: Part of the area known as the 'Wadis', which was very reminiscent of World War I trench warfare. /IWM

Right: A group of British Tommies enjoy a light meal before going into action./IWM

Below: Tanks of B Squadron, 46 RTR, move up for a counter-attack in the Nettuno area./IWM

by the long deep wadis, heavily overgrown, which changed hands nightly. A sort of grotesque hide-and-seek had been played for days in these wadis. The Irish would debouch from one particular wadi and assault an enemy held one, and on their return would sometimes find the Boche in occupation of their own positions. The Guardsmen were on top all right, but deadly tired. The real trouble was that the maps were useless; it was impossible to move by day and impossible to see by night, with the result that no one really knew where they were in the labyrinth of wadis.

'Meanwhile at the wadi later called "The Boot", because of its shape on the map, A and B companies had arrived and were taking over. The catastrophe, the fear of which had always lurked behind every relief, befell us that night. As the troops of both battalions were actually out in the open in the act of handing over the exiguous slit trenches, a concentration of heavy shells and mortar bombs crashed into "The Boot". Casualties were caused to both battalions and Noel Wimpenny (OC A Company) was half-dazed

by a near miss. The handover, which was bound anyway to be a sketchy proceeding, had to be hurried. It would have been madness to keep two sets of troops in a position where only dubious protection existed for one.

'The main body of the Irish Guards marched off and a few officers and NCOs remained behind to pass on what information they possessed to the distracted Dukes' officers, pushing their men into position in the blackness and locating the wounded by the moans. A few concentrations fell round the culvert, but fortunately did no damage to C Company (Capt Hall) which was taking over positions there. Andrew had done all he could, and during a lull in the shelling he moved off with his HQ. As he left he asked me to keep a particular eye on a Sgt Moriarty of the Irish Guards who had not left "The Boot" and who, Andrew said, had done particularly good work. At almost that moment the lifeless body of that gallant NCO was toppling into an empty slit trench; looking for a wounded man in the darkness he was hit by a fragment of mortar shell.'

Below: One of the thousands of propaganda leaflets dropped over the beachhead./*Adam Forty*

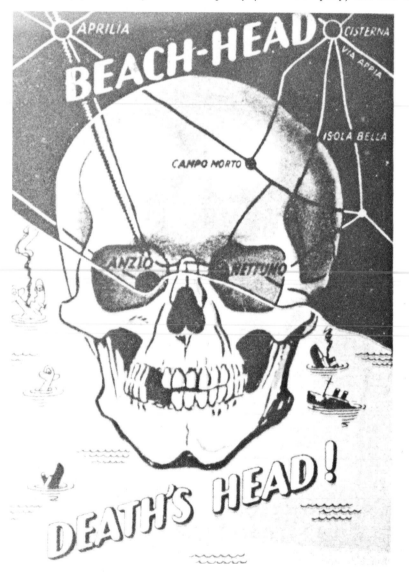

THE BEACH-HE

is going to be the big b
against the Germans.

Wasn't that the slogan of three months

TODAY

it is still a beach-head and nothing

but it is now paved with the skulls of tho
of British and American sold

The Beach-Head has
become a Death's Head!

It is welcoming You with a grin, and also
who are coming after you across the sea
appointment with death.

Do they know what they are in
Yes, they feel that they are landin

DEATH'S HEA

The American Eagle

Mark Wayne Clark, the son of Col Charles and Mrs Rebecca Clark, was born at Madison Barracks, New York on 1 May 1896. He began his army career just about as auspiciously as anyone could hope to, when no less a person than the President of the United States of America, helped him to get his appointment to West Point. President Woodrow Wilson was a friend of Mark Clark's aunt, Mrs Marshall, of Highland Park, Illinois, and thanks to his help the young man was accepted as the nomination from the Third District of New York. 'Opie', as he was called at the Military Academy – a nickname given to him as he always read a comic strip in a sunday newspaper that featured a character called Opie Dilldock – soon discovered that such attention from high places did not always 'win friends and influence people', when Dudley Field Malone, Assistant Secretary of State, visited West Point to review the cadets. Mark Clark, still a 'plebe' (ie: a junior cadet) was called out of the ranks to meet the VIP in front of the entire Academy. Upperclassmen clearly resented a newcomer hogging the limelight in this way and afterwards made him stand to attention for hours and hours in his room as a punishment! Nevertheless he did well at West Point, graduating in 1917. Here is how 'Opie' was described in the Class of 1917 copy of *The Howitzer*, which was (and still is) the yearbook that is published just before the graduation of each class at West Point:

'Opie has all the characteristics that go to make a versatile caydet, including a long string of "Opie" and a typical "A" Co walk or rather gait – it being a well-known fact that only the runts know how to walk. By the way, no rumor ever suffered the diminution of its pristine splendour from having passed through Opie's hands (or mouth). He is always careful to give out said rumour at least as good as it was when he got it. Occasionally he delves into hop life; then again he sallies forth from around the goats,* and soars up into the sacred precints of the first section, but he's so tall naturally that added height makes him dizzy and he slides right back again. On a hike during First Class Camp, Opie managed to get tangled up in an artillery chariot which

climbed a stone wall on two wheels, and as a result he missed the Fort Wright trip. His optimistic viewpoint of life in general remained unchanged, however, for Opie is bound for the Doughboys,† and "Who'd go in the Coast‡ anyway?" Furthermore, Opie is one of the class twins, for after a long and indecisive battle with Collins to determine which is the younger, it was decided to split the honors.'

† 'Doughboys' – the infantry.
‡ 'Coast' – refers to the Coast Artillery branch of the artillery.

* 'Goats' are cadets who are in the lower part of their class academically.

Below: Commanders and staff officers, Louisiana Army Manoeuvres, September 1941. Brig-Gen Mark Clark is pictured here with Col Dwight D. Eisenhower, Chief of Staff Third Army, behind (l to r) Brig-Gen Malony (Deputy COS GHQ), Gen Lear (CG Second Army), Gen Krueger (CG Third Army) and Gen McNair (COS GHQ)./*US Army*

Bottom: Commander of US Ground Forces in Europe. Mark Clark relaxes at his HQ in England./*IWM*

Above: Generals Clark and Eisenhower are pictured here standing in a captured German reconnaissance car, whilst attending a demonstration of mine clearance at the Fifth Army Engineer Training Centre in North Africa.
/Fifth Army Photo Unit

are well retold in Mrs Clark's book: *Captain's Bride, General's Lady*, published in 1956. After accompanying her husband on many tours abroad after the war, Mrs Maurine Clark sadly died in 1966. General Clark later remarried.

His rise to prominence really began when, in August 1940, he was named as Assistant Chief of Staff for Operations at the General Headquarters, US Army. This new HQ had been activated at the Army War College, Washington DC, in view of the desperate situation in Europe, with the Axis in the ascendancy and Great Britain in immediate danger of invasion. GHQ, under Gen George Marshall's expert guidance (he had been appointed Chief of Staff of the US Army on 1 September 1939), faced the monumental task of mobilising, organising and training the field forces within the continental USA.

The staff consisted of a remarkable group of officers, including such men as Gen Lesley J. McNair, who almost completely reorganised the system of training in the US Army and was responsible for most of the basic field force divisional organisations of the Army Ground Forces. Mark Clark became Deputy Chief of Staff of the Army Ground Forces, under Gen McNair, in January 1942 and four months later Chief of Staff, AGF. As one of the accompanying photographs shows, another notable member of the dedicated group of officers reponsible for training the emergent US Army, was a Colonel Dwight D. Eisenhower, who, after demonstrating his grasp of logisitics, strategy and tactics on such manoeuvres as those held in Louisiana in September 1941, not to mention his calm and friendly manner, was made Chief of Operations of the War Department General Staff in Washington in early 1942. Later that same year Eisenhower was named as the US commander in Europe. Gen Eisenhower's unique achievements as Supreme Allied Commander, first in North Africa and then in Europe, do not need repeating here. Two years senior to Mark Clark at West Point, they had nevertheless been in the same company, lived in the same division of barracks and had become firm friends. In his book *Crusade in Europe*, Eisenhower had this to say about meeting Mark Clark again:

'While serving in the 3rd Division, I renewed a friendship of my cadet days with Major Mark W. Clark. He and I worked together constantly in many phases of the field exercise we both so much enjoyed, and I gained a lasting respect for his planning, training and organising ability, which I have not seen excelled in any other officer.'

Graduating in April 1917 into the infantry, he was rapidly promoted from 2-Lt to 1-Lt (May 1917) and then to temporary captain (August 1917). Soon afterwards, he joined the 11th Infantry Regiment, to command Company K. They were part of the US 5th Infantry Division – the Red Diamond Division – then serving with the American Expeditionary Force in France. He had a brilliant war record in World War I, was wounded in action in the Vosges mountains, served on the staff of First Army, took part in both the St Mihiel and Meuse-Argonne offensives, and commanded an infantry battalion at the age of 22. After the war he served with Third Army, the American Army of Occupation in Germany. Returning to peacetime soldiering in the USA in 1919, Mark Clark had a varied run of assignments, graduating from the Infantry School at Fort Benning, Georgia, in 1925, and among other postings was an instructor for four years (1929-1933) with the Indiana National Guard. He married his first wife, Maurine Doran, at Washington Cathedral in May 1924 and they and their two children had the normal happy, hectic, if frustrating life, led by most regular army families between the wars. These days

In his book *Calculated Risk*, Gen Clark tells a splendid story about the first meeting that he and 'Ike' had with Field Marshal (then

General) Montgomery in May 1942. 'Monty' was then GOC of British troops in south-east England and had invited a party of American officers, including Clark and Eisenhower, over from the States to observe a series of manoeuvres, which he had aptly called 'Tiger'. Gen Montgomery's first briefing was crisp, clear and concentrated, and after a while Ike decided that he must have a cigarette to aid his concentration. He lit up, had time for a couple of puffs, when, sniffing the air without looking round from the briefing map, Monty icily inquired who was smoking. 'I am', said Ike meekly. 'I do not,' replied Monty sternly, 'permit smoking in my office.' Gen Eisenhower put out his cigarette, and he and Mark Clark had a good laugh about it later – but not, Gen Clark adds, until they were well out of Montgomery's hearing!

In June 1942, Mark Clark was assigned as Commanding General of II Corps in England, and took off from Bolling Field on 23 June. It would be five long years before he would return for duty in the United States. During this second visit to England Gen Clark met the Prime Minister, Winston Churchill. Mark Clark described Churchill as: 'the greatest man I have ever met', whilst Churchill was also clearly impressed by the 'American Eagle', as he nicknamed Mark Clark. It was to be through Churchill's later insistence that Gen Clark would take over command of 15th Army Group from Gen Alexander. In July 1942, Gen Clark was named as Commander of the US Army Ground Forces in the European Theatre of Operations and then, in the October of the same year, became Deputy C-in-C of the Allied Forces for the North Africa, with Ike as his C-in-C.

The first of these appointments involved him in the ground work of planning the vast organisational, housing and training programmes, for the US forces in Britain, whilst the latter gave him a leading part in planning the invasion of North Africa. It is not often that a general has the opportunity of landing on the beaches his troops will be invading *ahead* of their actual invasion, but that is exactly what Mark Clark did in October 1942. After flying to Gibraltar in a B-17 bomber called *The Red Gremlin*, he made a dramatic, hazardous, but sucessful trip in HM Submarine *Seraph*, to French North Africa, for a secret rendezvous with a group of French officers in order to coordinate details

Above left: Mark Clark enjoying a 'diffa' (a feast) given by the Caid El Ayadi. The caid was the leader of the Rohamna Arabs of Morocco and gave the feast for Gen Clark and his staff after a wolf hunt./*US Army*

Above: With Eisenhower. Mark Clark and his lifelong friend 'Ike' cheerfully discussing aspects of the Italian campaign – clearly things are going well for Fifth Army!/*US Army*

Below: Comparing profiles? 'The American Eagle' chatting with an RAF despatch rider (LAC T. Goodwin) at Fifth Army advanced command post in Italy./*IWM*

Right: Christmas at the front. Mark Clark personally delivering Christmas gift packages to two of his Fifth Army GIs./*US Army*

Below right: Visit of HM King George VI. HM inspects Fifth Army troops during a visit in July/August 1944. It was during this visit that he made the formal presentation of the KBE to Mark Clark./*IWM*

for the proposed Operation Torch landings. This secret, very dangerous mission clearly tested not only Gen Clark's considerable personal courage, but also his sense of humour, because on his safe return he was asked by HM King George VI to explain how he got stranded on the enemy beach minus his pants!

Mark Clark flew from Gibraltar to Algiers on the day following the landings. He immediately took into protective custody Admiral Darlan, Cabinet Minister in the German dominated Vichy French government and C-in-C of all French forces, who happened to be in Algiers visiting his sick son. After some tricky negotiations he was able to persuade Darlan to repudiate the Vichy regime and to order all French troops in NW and West Africa, to stop resisting the American and British forces. The negotiations were further complicated by trying to decide which senior French officer should be made 'Head of State' between Darlan and Gen Giraud, who had escaped from German captivity in April 1942 to France, and thence to Gib-

raltar, and was brought to North Africa by a British submarine in November 1942. 'I now have two grand-daddies on my hands', said Clark to Eisenhower, referring to Darlan and Giraud!

In January 1943, Gen Clark was designated Commanding General of the Fifth Army, the first American Army to be activated in the European theatre. The success of this appointment and his subsequent success as CG of the Fifteenth Army Group in Italy, are clearly demonstrated in the remaining pages of this book, so I will not detail them again here. Mark Clark showed himself to be a charismatic, forceful and successful field commander, who had the happy knack of being able to make his polyglot force work in harmony for most of the time! There was considerable mutual respect between Mark Clark and Alexander, and Gen Clark had implicit faith in his C-in-C's judgement and to quote his own words: 'above all in his fairness and his willingness to lay the cards right on the table. We could discuss frankly differences of opinion. I have never met a man who was a finer leader.'*

At the end of hostilities in Europe Mark Clark was appointed US High Commissioner in Austria and was the US member of the Allied Commission for Austria. In this capacity he rendered distinguished service, helping among other things to feed the people, restore and maintain law and order in Austria, weed out Nazis from public office and prepare the country for independence under a democratic self-government. In 1947 he was

* Quoted in *Alex;* Nigel Nicolson.

Left: Gen Clark visits Gen Vincenzo Dapino, commander of the 1st Italian Motorised Brigade, who were part of his Army./*US Army*

Above: With Fifth Army heroes. Mark Clark stands proudly beside three of his soldiers who have just been decorated – the centre GI wears the Congressional Medal of Honor (USA's highest decoration for bravery), whilst the other two wear Distinguished Service Crosses./*US Army*

Right: Mark Clark uses a map to describe the dispositions of his Fifth Army to Maj-Gen Eurico Gaspar Dutra, Brazil's Minister of War. The 1st Brazilian Division who fought with Fifth Army, were the first Brazilian troops ever to fight in Europe./*IWM*

deputy to the US Secretary of State and sat in both London and Moscow with the Council of Foreign Ministers, negotiating a peace treaty for Austria. His first 'home posting' for five years came in June 1947, when he was appointed CG of the Sixth Army with headquarters at the Presido of San Francisco, California. Two years later he was appointed Chief of the Army Field Forces at Fort Monroe, Virginia and held that appointment for three years. Then he was off on his travels once more, this time to the Far East to become Commander in Chief, United Nations Command, Commanding General US Forces Far East and Governor of the Ruyku Islands – an island chain in the West Pacific between Japan and Taiwan – taking up all these appointments on 12 May 1952. During his command, he signed, on 27 July 1953, the military armistice agreement between the United Nations Command and the military commanders of the North Korean Army and

Above: Gen Clark receives the ribbon of the Knight Commander of the Most Excellent Order of the British Empire from Gen Sir Harold Alexander, C-in-C Italy, at a ceremony on 29 April 1944. /IWM

Left: Mark Clark pictured here in his jeep, during a visit to British units of Fifth Army. He is accompanied by Lt-Gen Kirkham, commander 13 Corps, whose divisions included British, Indian and South African troops. On this occasion Gen Clark is not accompanied by his cocker spaniel 'Pal', who normally went everywhere with him. /IWM

Below left: The Big Boss visits. Mark Clark talks with two British generals during a flying visit from his Fifteenth Army headquarters. The suitably inscribed Piper Cub stands ready for take off. Gen Clark had some hair raising flights during his time with Fifth Army – for example, during a visit to the Anzio beachhead, the plane's pontoons (fitted so that it could land in the sea) were badly damaged. They finally had to crash land on the beach at Sorrento, the plane being 'fit only for the salvage heap' afterwards! /IWM

Left: Allied generals at Hitler's home. Mark Clark, accompanied by Gen McCreery (Britain), Gen Bethouart (France) and Gen Zheltov (Russia), sign the big conference table at Hitler's 'Eagles Nest', 20 August 1945./*IWM*

Below: Victory Parade in Vienna. Gen Mark Clark, Gen Winterton, Gen Kuresov and Gen Joppe, take the salute before inspecting Allied troops in Vienna, 8 May 1945./*IWM*

the Chinese People's Volunteers, at Munsan-ni, Korea. Gen Clark's military service came to an end in October 1953, when he relinquished his three posts, returned to the USA and retired from the Army on 31 October at his own request. Since retiring Gen Clark has been President of 'The Citadel', the Military College of South Carolina, located in Charleston.

I would like to close this short chapter with some anecdotes which, I believe, show well the very human qualities of this outstanding soldier. I think that they clearly demonstrate that not only does he possess a considerable sense of humour – even when the joke is on him – but also show him to be a warm hearted and generous person, always prepared to give credit where it is due. The first was recounted by his late wife in her book and concerns an incident during a short holiday which they spent together at Palm Beach, when Gen Clark was visiting USA for the 'Victory in Europe' celebrations in Chicago. They went for a ride one balmy evening, using the Government-supplied jeep, Gen Clark in his olive drab service trousers, shirt minus insignia and his wife in a light summer dress. He had taken off his envelope-type overseas cap and they drove happily along the beach road until they were stopped by two zealous young Military Policemen. 'You've got a government vehicle here buddy and a dame in it – let's see your trip ticket!' None could be produced, so, whilst the MPs were looking in their own jeep for some charge sheets, Mark Clark took the opportunity of hastily jamming on his headgear, with its four glistening stars (denoting full General). The young MPs were transfixed and full of embarrassed apologies. Gen Clark asked for their names and unit, and they left, convinced that they were for the high jump. Instead, he commended them to their commander for doing their job so thoroughly: 'I wish you could have seen those two lads, sir,' said their CO later, 'They thought they were to be torn apart for arresting you and were completely floored when I told them of your commendation.'

The second story was sent to me by General Albert Gruenther, who was Mark Clark's Chief of Staff throughout the Italian campaign. After reminding me that Gen Clark will be 83 this May (1979), he wrote:
'Speaking of his age, I had an interesting experience with him when our Fifth Army headquarters was in Morocco in May 1943. I understood that he enjoyed being congratulated on his 1 May birthday, so I decided to have some fun with him on that day. The plan: no one was to congratulate him on his birthday. I started by enrolling Sergeant Chaney, an assistant of his, who would awaken him. But Sgt Chaney was most reluctant to participate. Finally he agreed to say "Good morning, General. It is a beautiful day." I had issued an order that a General "X" (I forget the name I used) would lecture the entire staff at 9.30am on the progress of the Tunisian operation. But by 9.30am, General Clark was in a cantankerous frame of mind. His friend, Gen Eisenhower, had not called him. Two of his West Point classmates, both staff members, had transacted business with him, but neither had said "Happy Birthday". About 9.00am, he called me to his office and said that he had to make an inspection trip and could not attend the lecture. I had anticipated that problem and I had the pilot report the plane out of order. So at 0930 he did show up for the lecture. As I was introducing the imaginary General X, a military clerk came up to me and interrupted me to say: "I have a message for General Clark". I waved him aside and continued with the introduction. Whereupon Gen Clark stood up at his front row seat and stated: "Let me have that message now." I then said: "Bring in the message". Two Red Cross girls appeared and sang "Happy Birthday Dear General". The meeting was then adjourned and an announcement was made that a small ceremony would take place on the adjoining square. That passed off pleasantly and everyone was happy. General Clark was in good humour again and that was his natural attitude.'

The final story is recounted by Mark Clark himself in his book *Calculated Risk* and refers to the ubiquitous Sgt Chaney, who was the general's personal orderly throughout the war, was decorated for bravery at Anzio, and served such famous personages as Winston Churchill and King George VI, 'with as much nonchalance as he turned out a plate of beans for a hungry lieutenant!' Gen Clark decided that he would make the award of the Good Conduct Medal as a Christmas gift for Chaney during their first Christmas in Italy. Unfortunately, when the suitable moment came for the presentation Chaney couldn't be found. 'He wasn't there,' Mark Clark explains, 'and I had just started to call for him when I heard a squeaky, off-key voice outside the tent, wavering uncertainly through a few bars of *Silent Night*. Everybody paused to listen, and then I let the Good Conduct Medal clatter on the table, Chaney was as drunk as a goat.' The general helped to put the sergeant to bed and then he and his guests settled down to eat the excellent dinner which Chaney had prepared before he started to celebrate. Some hours later, when Chaney had recovered his equilibrium, Gen Clark got him into the tent, 'propped him up in the corner', made a suitable speech and pinned the medal on his orderly's chest!

Breaking the Gustav Line

The French Break Through

'Darkness settled slowly over the Gargliano River on the evening of 11 May. The day had been cloudy, and a little rain had fallen. After sunset, smoke and haze still blanketed the valley, but the vast canopy of stars shone down brightly from a clear sky. Except for the crash of an occasional artillery piece all was still. Long columns of swarthy French colonial troops and laden mules moved softly along the steep trails and roads leading to the Mt Juga bridgehead. On the lines of departure the infantry stirred restlessly. The enemy came out of his hiding places and went unsuspectingly about his tasks of strengthening fortifications, patrolling and bringing up supplies. All was normal, as it had been to German eyes and ears for the past month.'*

From Salerno to the Alps; ed Chester G. Starr.

For the past two months the battle for Rome had been bogged down, both around the seemingly impregnable fortress of Cassino and at the Anzio beachhead, where the expected breakout had still not been achieved. The 'soft underbelly of Europe' was certainly turning out to be not as soft as had been expected! However, if the Italian campaign was to be got moving again, then the Allies must find a way of resuming the offensive, and that necessitated a major regrouping. Accordingly, most of the Eighth Army front was stripped down to the bare minimum, whilst a peninsular-wide regrouping took place, under a cloak of the strictest secrecy, as the Eighth Army divisions were redeployed west of the Apennines. 'Diadem' was the codeword chosen for this spring offensive and one of its key features was to be a bold 'push' through the mountains, where the Germans would be least

Below: Gen de Monsabert, commander of 3rd Algerian Infantry Division moves his command post forward./*ECP Armées*

79

expecting attack. This was the brainchild of General Alphonse Juin, commander of the French Expeditionary Corps (FEC). The original Fifth Army plan had proposed an advance along the relatively good going of the Ausente valley, whilst Gen Juin proposed to attack directly through the mountains, making no attempt to outflank the Mte Aurunci feature. Gen Mark Clark was attracted by the boldness of Juin's plan and agreed to it. The first essential was to break out of the Gargliano bridgehead, then the FEC would take Mte Majo and the Ausonia defile, while II Corps gained control of the hills north of Minturno overlooking the southern end of the Ausonia valley. The French would then drive straight across the valley into the Petrella massif, assisted by II Corps at Mte la Civita and Spigno. Both corps would then fan out and seize the lower ground to the flanks so as to advance their front onto the Itri-Pico road. All divisions of Fifth Army, less 36 Division, who were the Army reserve, would be committed to the attack. Surprise and aggression were to be the keynotes, instead of slugging slowly forward, they would smash the enemy with one fierce blow and crack him wide open. Undoubtedly the 'clincher' in making such an attack a success was Juin's FEC. It consisted of the traditional French Army of Africa – Tirailleurs, Goums and Spahis, an élite force under a renowned and beloved commander. Juin said of these troops, 'I adored them because I had trekked with them in Morocco.' The FEC had started to arrive in Italy in November 1943 and were now complete. Gen Juin's first order of the day on landing had been a clarion call to French honour:

'The hour we have been waiting for has struck at last! The battlefields of Italy are open before you and you are called upon to fight at the side of our valiant allies for the liberation of our country. You will give proof of the faith which inspires you. The eyes of suffering France are fixed upon you.'

They had certainly vindicated his faith in their bravery, for in late January, the Tirailleurs of 3rd Algerian Division had forded the Rapido through waist deep, swirling, icy water, and captured Mte Belvedere after fierce hand-to-hand fighting. Juin wrote later of this action: 'I do not think that there has ever been a more brilliant feat of arms in the annals of the French Army.' Now the presence of his knife-wielding mountain troops would make all the difference between the success and failure of the new offensive. H-Hour for 'Diadem' was fixed at 2300 hours 11 May 1944, set at that time so as to give the attackers a chance to break through the enemy defences in darkness and then to have plenty of moonlight for their exploitation, as moonrise

Left: Stuck in the mud! A French jeep negotiates the sticky mud of a swollen stream on the way to Ausonia. /ECP Armées

Centre left: The FEC advance. Mountain troops of the French Expeditionary Corps move forward, carrying their artillery and heavy weapons on mules. /ECP Armées

Bottom left: De Gaulle visits. Gen de Gaulle visits the FEC during the May offensive. In the rear of the jeep is the commander of the FEC, Gen Alphonse Juin. /ECP Armées

Right: Gen de Lattre de Tassigny pictured here during the visit by Gen de Gaulle to the FEC – what a traffic jam! /ECP Armées

Below: French troops cover German prisoners as they are taken for interrogation at the 'Bureau de Renseignements' (the Intelligence Office) in Ausonia, which they captured on 15 May 1944. /ECP Armées

was half an hour later. Gen Juin had chosen the 2nd Moroccan Infantry Division, known as the 'FEC's battering ram' under command of Gen Dody, for the breakout and capture of Mte Majo and its three spurs (Mte Feuci, Mte Cerasola and Mte Girofano). On the right was 1st Free French Division (1 DFL) under Gen Brosset, maintaining contact with the Eighth Army. On the left was the redoubtable 3rd Algerian Infantry Division under Gen de Monsabert, which had the important task of taking the key position of Castleforte which would open the Ausente valley to the advance. Once this first phase had been successfully completed, the Mountain Corps of the 4th Moroccan Mountain Division (4 DMM) under Gen Savez and the Berber mountaineers (the Group of Moroccan Tabors, the Goums) under Gen Guillame, would make its way to the Aurunci massif. The corps would drive straight across the 10-mile deep, 4,600ft high feature and cut the Itri-Pico road.

'Suddenly at 2300 the guns roared into action. Great flashes burst up from the hills and hundreds of shells screamed across the Gargliano. The crash and roar swept down the line through II Corps to the sea. The mountains across the river became an inferno of exploding shells and bursting flares. The ridges were outlined briefly, faded quickly from sight, and then came into view again and again. Throughout the night and the following day more than 1,000 guns roared from Cassino to the sea. Of these, 600 were massed under the control of Fifth Army; during the first 24 hours of the attack, our artillery fired 173,941 rounds against the enemy. The effect of this savage, concentrated smash was overwhelming, Enemy batteries were tossed in ruins; routes of supply were pitted by shell holes; command posts disappeared from the web of German communications. The mass of information which we had piled up about the Gustav Line had been used to give the enemy a number of surprises on D-Day. When the sun rose on 12 May, our air force began its operations to isolate the battlefield. Though cloudy weather seriously interfered with these efforts, our pilots reported fair results. In addition to 294 fighter bomber sorties, 429 medium bomber sorties were flown on communications behind enemy lines. In the heavy bomber class 728 sorties hit at communications and other targets. Kesselring's HQ was attacked twice during the day, and the bombs of 80 heavy bombers completely destroyed Tenth Army HQ. Continuation of this pounding day after day brought a cumulative effect which hampered the enemy severely and made his ruin more certain!'*

In the darkness, waiting for the barrage to finish, the men of the 'FEC battering ram' began moving from their assembly areas on Mte Juga towards their assault positions on the eastern slopes of Mte Majo, there to wait for about half an hour while the guns pumped shells into the German positions on the rocky slopes above. Unfortunately, as was found on other occasions, the Allied firepower did not

* *From Salerno to the Alps;* ed Chester G. Starr.

Below: Covered with a generous layer of Italian dust, a jeep load of French troops move through the small village of Vallicorsa./*ECP Armées*

cause as many casualties as the weight of shells might have suggested. The German commander, Gen Raapke, warned by the unusually heavy registration of targets the week before, had had the good sense to move much of his artillery to alternate positions, so that the Allied fire inflicted few casualties to his batteries. Many of the well protected infantry dugouts were also relatively unscathed as they were too close to the French lines to be hit. The main effects of the barrage were undoubtedly the disrupting of line communications and the isolation of scattered infantry positions. During the first two hours of the attack, the Moroccan infantry fought their way to within 300yd of the 2,000ft summit of Mte Ornito, some two miles south-east of the main divisional objective. No sooner had they reached their new positions than they were counter-attacked. By midmorning on the 12th they had fought their way to the crest of Mte Faito, but were still over a mile short of the main objective, which Juin had confidently expected to take within the first five hours of the attack. German defenders had also thwarted a supporting attack on the right aimed at clearing positions on the Cerasola Hill–Hill 739–Mte Garfano complex, which overlooked the route which the Moroccans must take to Mte Majo. Despite this failure Gen Dody still tried to press forward, but his troops were quickly halted by withering fire from the heights. Hearing of the setback, Gen Juin left his HQ and moved forward despite the rough going, heavy enemy mortar fire and other difficulties. He reached the top of Mte

Above: An enemy mine explodes on the road to the village of Castro de Volsci, during the FEC drive./ECP Armées

Left: Two crew members help their tank commander to an aid station after he was wounded by a mine on the outskirts of Vallicorsa. Note the interesting mixture of headgear – US tank crew helmets, French and British steel helmets./ECP Armées

Ornito, from which vantage point he had a good view of the battle area. 'On reaching the top,' said Juin, 'I found Colonels Gallies and Molle who made no secret of the fact that it was tough going. The enemy were counter-attacking Monte Faito. I observed, however, that our artillery was very active and that the German reserves were being battered by our 400 guns. I concluded that the attack should be resumed.'*

General Juin's confidence soon revitalised his flagging troops and in a few hours the attack was restarted as Col Starr relates in his history of Fifth Army:

'At 0320 on 13 May, all artillery attached to Dody's division, except for two battalions supporting the troops on Monte Faito, began to fire on Cerasola Hill. Forty minutes later, as the reserve regiment began to advance, the artillery fire shifted to Hill 739 and finally to Mte Garofano. At the last minute before the Moroccan infantry began their ascent, a detachment of combat engineers rushed forward with bangalore torpedoes to blow gaps in barbed wire blocking the path of the advance. The artillery apparently did its job well, for as the riflemen climbed the slope, German reaction was almost nonexistent. Reducing the few positions that had escaped the bombardment, the Moroccans moved quickly on to the next objective, Hill 739 and then onto the third, Monte Garofano. Within two and a half hours the regiment had occupied all three objectives, capturing 150 enemy soldiers in the process, and even advanced a few hundred yards farther to occupy yet another hill mass overlooking the village of Vallomajo in the shadow of Monte Majo. Success was not so readily achieved on the left, where the regiment making the 2nd Moroccans main effort tried to get moving shortly after 0400, first toward an intermediate objective, Monte Feuci, about midway between Mte Faito and the objective, then on to Mte Majo. Almost immediately the regiment ran into a counter-attack by the 71st Division's lone reserve battalion. Even though the Moroccans held, employing mortar and artillery fire to deadly effect to drive the Germans back, the action checked the French advance.

'Three more times before daylight and again at 0900 the German battalion tried to recapture Mte Faito with no success. Now the French, rather than the Germans, occupied the high ground on the right which hampered the counter-attacks from Mte Feuci just as it had hampered French efforts to attack that feature. French gunners, with the observation advantage that daylight brought, had turned the last counter-attack into a

costly failure. Broken by heavy casualties, the enemy battalion fell back in disorder. Covered by an artillery preparation, the Moroccan infantrymen reached the crest of Mte Feuci by 1130; not a shot was fired against them. The destruction of Raapke's reserve battalion, after the heavy punishment the troops in the main line of resistance had already taken, meant that no means existed for holding the Monte Majo sector of the Gustav Line. As the French regrouped, a radio operator intercepted a German radio message saying: "Feuci has fallen. Accelerate the general withdrawal". When a platoon-sized patrol left Mte Feuci a few minutes later to test German defences on Monte Majo, the results appeared to confirm the German message, for the patrol found not a German there. In late afternoon a battalion came forward to occupy the objective and to raise on an improvised flagstaff a French tricolour large enough to be seen from Monte Cassino to the Tyrrhenian Sea.

'Breaking through to Mte Majo on 13 May, the Moroccans had breached the Gustav Line at one of its deepest, albeit most weakly defended, points. The feat had unhinged the entire left wing of the XIV Panzer Corps. It had also split Gen Raapke's 71st Division and opened the way for further advances along the parallel ridges running northwest towards Ausonia, San Giorgio and Esperia and for a thrust across the Ausonia defile to Monte Fammera.'

Kesselring wrote later: 'Thenceforth there was no stopping the French advance. The French units were used to mountain work and could go where they liked.' The road to Rome had at last been opened!

The First Test

'It was a quiet, lazy spring day. The date was 11 May but outwardly it was no different from any other day on that front. Fields of scarlet poppies nodded and bobbed in a faint sea breeze; smoke pots at the Minturno bridge drifted an acrid haze across the valley; an incoming shell punctuated the stillness now and then with a muttering crash. South of Minturno, the men of the Vampire Platoon – so named because it had bivouacked in a cemetery, sleeping by day and gliding about the front by night – made last checks of their equipment, slept a little, wrote letters or talked about the job ahead of them. There was not much to say. Even the trite phrase "This is it!" had lost its original humour, for this really was it. And no joking about it. Daylight faded and dancing stars winked across a clear sky. A dog howled somewhere, its cry echoing over the silent valley. Mimosa drenched the night air with a nostalgic perfume. The minutes crept on. It was 2230.

---

* *The War Lords;* ed FM Sir Michael Carver.

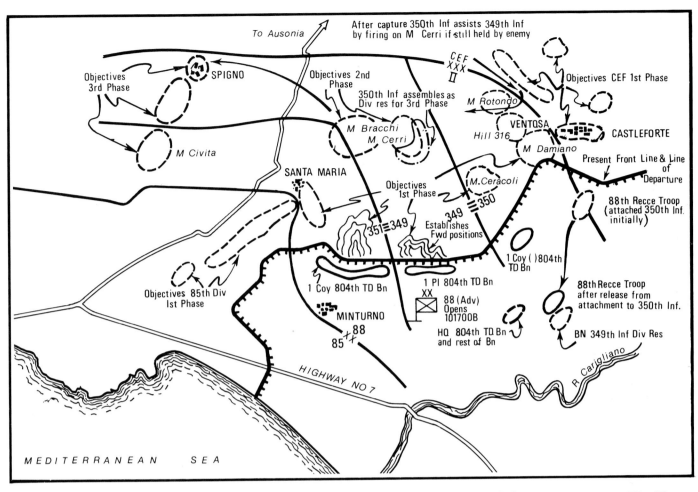

Labels on map:

To Ausonia

After capture 350th Inf assists 349th Inf
by firing on M Cerri if still held by enemy

Objectives
3rd Phase

SPIGNO

Objectives 2nd
Phase

350th Inf assembles as
Div res for 3rd Phase

M Rotondo

CEF
XXX
II

Objectives CEF 1st Phase

M Bracchi
M Cerri

VENTOSA

Hill 316

CASTLEFORTE

M Civita

M Damiano

SANTA MARIA

Present Front Line & Line
of
Departure

M.Ceracoli

Objectives
1st Phase

350

88th Recce Troop
(attached 350th Inf.
initially)

351 349

349

Establishes
Fwd positions

1 Coy ( )804th
TD Bn

Objectives 85th Div
1st Phase

1 Coy 804th TD Bn

1 Pl 804th TD Bn

XX

88 (Adv)
Opens
101700B

88th Recce Troop
after release from
attachment to 350th Inf.

MINTURNO

88

85 XX

HQ 804th TD Bn
and rest of Bn

BN 349th Inf Div Res

R. Carigliano

HIGHWAY NO 7

MEDITERRANEAN SEA

And then 2245 – 2255. It was 2300 – H-hour of D-Day. Attack! A solid leaping sheet of flame shattered the stillness of the night as the greatest artillery concentration since El Alamein roared sudden death out of the darkness into German lines. From coast to coast along the long-dormant front, uncounted tons of steel spat from the throats of roaring American, English, French, Canadian and Polish guns. This was the spring push.

'Silently, quickly, from their sangars and dugouts the men of the 88th took their first few steps on what was to be a long and bloody and bitter trail, began doing the job for which they had been trained so well, began making battle history. Part of the strategy to keep the Germans ignorant of the push until the last possible minute called for no advance artillery preparation. Shells and men moved at the same instant with the men following the savage barrage as closely as possible. Stunned at first by the ferocity of the barrage which came hurling at them from the once deceptively quiet Gargliano River flats, the Germans nevertheless were quick to react. They poured a murderous hail of mortar and small-arms fire down the slopes at the advancing doughboys who were battering at their sector of the Gustav Line. Front-line units passed the word back to rear headquarters that this attack was the big one.

German heavy batteries at Gaeta turned their guns inshore and tried for the Minturno Bridge to cut what they knew was our main supply route. The Krauts fought back but there was no stopping our initial surge. In less that 51 minutes Mt Damiano, key to the defences and a height which Gen Clark had boasted could be taken whenever the 88th desired, had fallen to the 350th Infantry Regiment. Capture of Damiano, or Cianelli as it was also called, passed almost unnoticed in news dispatches at the time but it was described later as one of the most outstanding operations in the initial assault on the Gustav Line. Its seizure covered the flank of the French Corps and enabled the French to crack through the bottleneck that was Castelforte, nicknamed "Little Cassino" by its conquerors.

'Individual exploits were numerous in that first clash and out of the smoke and flame came a young Irish lad who was destined to become the first man in the Division to merit the Medal of Honor. The lad was S/Sgt Charles W. "Red" Shea of the Bronx, New York, and the 350th, a one time peanut butcher at Yankee Stadium. Whilst going over the crest of Diamiano shortly after dawn, Shea's platoon leader was killed and his platoon sergeant wounded. Taking cover from enemy artillery, Shea spotted two trip wires at his head and feet; realised he was in the middle of a minefield. A Kraut machine gun opened up on the men trapped in the field. Shea realized it had to be silenced. Without hesitation he rose and started for the gun. As he approached the position, some sixth sense warned him to turn. He whirled about to see a German emerging from another machine gun position, and pointing a machine pistol at him. Shea levelled his rifle and the Kraut surrendered. Four other Germans emerged from the position. One refused to come out. Motioning with his rifle, Shea directed the PWs to return to the rear – one died when he stepped on a mine. The last Kraut in the position rose to toss a grenade at an officer leading another platoon and Shea got him with one shot. Manoeuvring now to keep out of range of the gunner he'd started out to get, Shea suddenly found himself directly beneath another machine gun nest, "so close I could have reached up and touched the barrel". He captured two more Krauts in this emplacement. The remaining Jerry was now the only problem. Suddenly this Kraut stood upright and fired eight shots from a P38 at Shea from less than 15 yards – and missed. Shea pulled off eight rounds from his rifle, and also missed. Both Yank and Kraut ducked for cover. Shea waited, another clip in his rifle. He spotted the German a few moments later, blood streaming down one side of his face as he rose to toss a grenade. Shea fired. Dying, the Kraut heaved his potato-masher but it was his last futile gesture.

'Things were rougher on the left side of the line. As the 350th mopped up on Damiano, the 351st butted against the stone wall that was Sante Maria Infante, a pivotal point in the Gustav Line left flank. With tanks, which knocked out 21 German machine guns in the first few hours, the 351st jumped off for Santa Maria with the 2nd Battalion in the lead. A hell of small-arms, machine gun and mortar fire caught the doughboys as they started up the rocky slopes. E Company led the assault on the right, F Company took the left and G Company was held in reserve. Early on 12 May F overcame resistance from Hill 130 and continued its advance up the terrain feature known as "The Tits", pulling abreast of E. Its commander wounded, E was held up on the spur. When Col Kendall's radio was knocked out by shellfire he moved up to determine the cause of the delay and assumed command of E on arrival. Spotting two machine guns, Col Kendall led an attack on one of the pillboxes. This gun was knocked out and Kendall then swung the company to the right under heavy mortar and machine gun fire. Moving up to the right of the "Tits", the outfit was stopped again by machine guns firing from flanks and front. Again Col

Left: High in a mountain sangar an artillery observation officer keeps a good watch for likely targets. Note the excellent shot of a Browning Automatic Rifle leaning against the rocks (also ration boxes!)./*US Army*

Below left: Fifth Army machine gunners engage a German patrol west of Fondi during the 'Diadem' offensive 11 May 1944. /*US Army*

Right: A rifle squad of US Rangers engage the enemy in the Santa Maria sector, as other squads assault. /*US Army*

Below: Allied vehicles, under cover of a smokescreen, slash through the Gustav Line. Leading vehicle over the bridge is a British universal carrier. /*IWM*

Kendall took off, this time with a squad from 24 Platoon and started for the gun which was firing from a position in a stone house to the right. First building up all the firepower possible and joining in the firefight himself with a carbine, bazooka, BAR and M1 with anti-tank grenades, Kendall then led the final assault on the house. As he pulled the pin of a hand grenade preparatory to throwing it, he was hit, by machine gun bullets from the left flank, receiving mortal wounds. Unable to throw the grenade, he held it to his stomach and fell with it to prevent injury to his men. The first of the original 88th battalion commanders was gone. An artillery liaison officer, 1-Lt Pat G. Coombs of the 913th, assumed command of the company after the death of Kendall and personally led the doughboys as they attacked and silenced three machine guns. He then ordered part of the unit to dig in while he and the remainder drove forward to capture the spur. During the battle Lt

Above: Rough going in Italy. Field artillery of the US 85th Division moves up a steep hill in the wake of the retreating Germans. /*US Army*

Left: American AFVs enter a small ruined town during the 'Diadem' offensive, 14 May 1944. The leading vehicle is an M10 Tank Destroyer, closely followed by a Sherman M4 medium tank./*US Army*

Above right: Backbone of the US field artillery. A 105mm Howitzer M2A1 engages the enemy from a position just outside a small Italian town. /*US Army*

Right: Allied bulldozers and motorised vehicles halt temporarily on their way up to the frontline along Highway 6, while two other dozers carry out some hasty repairs so that the column can move on again./*IWM*

Coombs maintained radio communication with his artillery and conducted effective supporting fire. When reinforcements moved up the Texan exposed himself to fire from both sides to identify his troops to the new outfit. . . .

'In the 351st, they were too busy to do much wondering about success or failure. The 1st Battalion, ordered to attack at 1600 hours 13 May, was taken over by Col Champeny when the battalion commander was separated from his unit while on reconnaissance. And stern, greying Col Champeny proved himself to his men as they lay pinned down under a barrage. Standing erect, apparently unmindful of the shells falling in his vicinity the colonel calmly directed operations – shouted words of encouragement to his bewildered doughboys. "It was magnificent" said Larry Newman, International News Service correspondent, who had been travelling with the 351st since the jumpoff. "We wanted to lie down and stay there, but with the Old Man standing up like a rock you couldn't stay down. Something about him just brought you right up to your feet. The guys saw him too. They figured if the Old Man could do it so could they. And when the time came they got up off the ground and started on again to Santa Maria." Early on the 14th the 1st Battalion took Hill 109 after considerable resistance which included traversing an extensive minefield and beating off a strong enemy counter-attack. Its flank wide open because Hill 131 was not taken on schedule, the battalion left the regimental zone and took 131 itself. During the actions of the morning Col Champeny spotted a Kraut artillery battery in position about 400yd from the crest of a hill. Under fire, he moved to a company position. Inspired by the Colonel, who again stood upright in the face of enemy machine gun fire, the men left the cover they had previously sought and over-ran the battery, killing and capturing a hundred Krauts. . . .

'In the first days of the push, the Recon Troop made its bid for glory with the capture of Mt Cerri by a 13 man patrol. During the months of the quiet war, recon patrols up the Ausente Valley always had met fire and resistance from Cerri and 2-Lt Lawrence (Cookie) Bowers of Grand Island, Nebraska, swore that some day he'd "get the Krauts on that damned hill." Shortly after 0200 hours 14 May, he and his little group of dismounted cavalrymen snipped the concertina wire at the base of the hill and crawled over a booby-trap wire. "We made it," said Sgt Leonard L. Juby of Boonville, New York, "but a couple of hours some of the fellows tripped it. Three of them were killed." Once over that obstacle, the men worked up a draw toward the Kraut machine gun covering the wire, found the position empty but could hear two Nazis talking as they went ahead of the Yanks up the hill. "Then we had to scale some cliffs just like infantry," said Cpl Vito V. Zaliagris of Detroit, Michigan, "and when we got to the top in regular squad formation the artillery was bursting all around us and the Krauts were scrambling down the other side. Me and Evaristo Alvarado just hugged the ground and prayed." While they were praying, Cookie sent Wayne W. Mills of Henderson, Texas and Cpl Barrett of Venita, Oklahoma – Barrett bagged five prisoners during the night – back down the hill to bring up the rest of the gang. By dawn the 350th had occupied and garrisoned the hill and the Recons withdrew. The Recons were justifiably proud and just a bit smug, about capturing what had been listed as a battalion objective.

'Action in the 350th sector had been favourable. The advance was swift and resistance was quickly overcome. By the morning of the 13th, both Hill 316 and Mt Ceracoli were taken, and at 1320 hours Gen Kendall, who was directing operations of all units in the Damiano area, reported that Ventosa had fallen to complete the action in the first phase by the 350th. One of the highlights came when an entire German battalion was caught in an assembly area by TOT (Time on Target) fire from the 337th, 338th, 339th and 918th Field Artillery Battalions. The shoot was such a success that observers later said there was no describing the scene of carnage that had been the Kraut assembly area. The 349th, held back as a reserve striking force, sent its 1st Battalion to occupy first phase objectives. These positions, involving a limited advance, were occupied at 0030 hours 12 May and the regiment awaited further orders. On the afternoon of the 14th, the 1st Battalion jumped off for Mt Bracchi and occupied it with A and B Companies by nightfall. But with Santa Maria fallen, the German Gustav Line was smashed, ripped wide open. The Nazis, fighting desperately for time, began a general withdrawal, the beginning of a retreat which did not stop completely until the Krauts had back-pedalled to their Gothic Line high in the Apennines. German prisoners, stumbling through the rubble heaps that had been their "impregnable" Gustav Line fortifications, were dazed and bewildered and glad to be alive; amazed at the savagery of the attacks hurled at them so suddenly out of the night. They had expected a spring drive – it was inevitable that there would be one. But they had not expected it so soon. Their commanders had told them that 24 May was the Fifth Army D-Day. That day had come 13 days too soon for them. They told PW interrogators that Yank troops – 88th troops – who swarmed in on their positions were on top of them within seconds after the artillery lifted. And they said that those men, those bearded, dirty, tired, angry, charging men with the blue Cloverleaf insignia, "fought like devils". The nodding poppy fields added new patches of red to their scarlet banks. The new red was blood. The breeze still carried the sweet fragrance of mimosa but along with that odour was a new scent, the unforgettable smell of the dead. The smoke pots at the Minturno Bridge no longer covered the valley with haze. Once again a man could walk upright, in broad daylight, across the Gargliano. And back in the Division Cemetery at Carano where the cost of the new push was counted in new white crosses, his notes for a book lay in the new grave with Frederick Faust, killed in the first hour of the push with many of the men he had wanted to write about at Santa Maria. That was the Gustav Line. That was the first test.'*

* *The Blue Devils in Italy;* John P. Delaney.

The Drive to Rome

Breakout from Anzio

'At about dusk 25 May 1944, a rather slack-appearing German officer, wearing a lieutenant-colonel's uniform, appeared in the interrogation room at the 3rd Infantry Division's cage just south of Borgo Montello, on what had been the Anzio beachhead. He was the commanding officer of the 955th Infantry Regiment, which had been charged with the defence of the city of Cisterna di Littoria and its immediate environs. At this moment his regiment no longer existed as a fighting force; Cisterna was in United States hands, and only small, disorganised groups and individual soldiers were falling back in front of our forces, or fleeing in an effort to reach previously selected areas and reorganise. The presence of the German lieutenant-colonel in our cage was symbolic of the two salient facts of the second battle of Cisterna; first, the tactics of the German defenders, which were to defend the place and face the alternatives of destruction; second, the total triumph of the Division's attack, which had in three days fulfilled that portion of the familiar

directive contained in the field order for the operation which read: "To destroy the enemy in the Division's zone of action".'*

During the Anzio breakout operation – called 'Buffalo' – there were many acts of individual heroism and I have chosen a few of those contained in the US 3rd Infantry Division's account of their battle for Cisterna. Company I of 30th Infantry reached its objective at the Ponte Rotto road junction, south-west of Cisterna, seven hours ahead of time and with their radio out of order. Friendly artillery was falling all round them as no one knew the company was so far ahead of schedule. In addition, enemy fire from an 88mm and three machine guns, plus a large group of infantry riflemen, all under 300yd away, was making life very unpleasant. S/Sgt Cleo A. Toothman recalled:
'We had been sitting there for about 30 minutes, helpless, unable to do a thing about

* *History of the 3rd Infantry Division;* ed Donald G. Taggart.

Below: Map 11 The plan of attack against Cisterna, 22 May 1944.

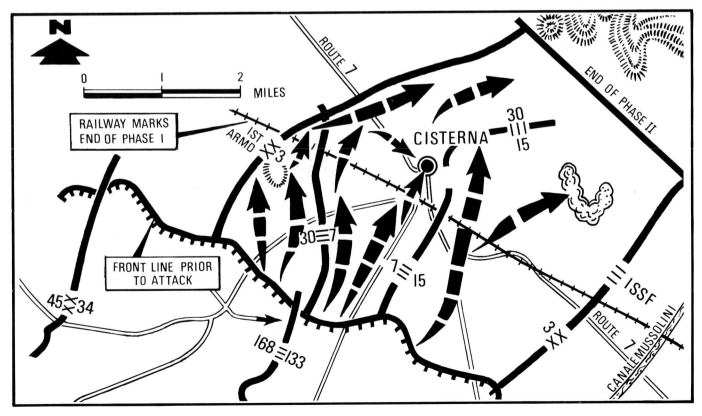

Above: On the road to Rome. American jeeps roll through the archway of what was an ancient Italian castle on the outskirts of Cisterna. */US Army*

the situation, when the BAR man in my squad, Pfc John Dutko, shouted to me, "Toothman, I'm going to get that 88 with my heater!" He always called his BAR his "Heater". Before I could say a word he took off like a ruptured duck. He made the first hundred yards in a dead run. Machine gun bullets were striking the ground only a foot or two behind him but he was running faster than the krauts could traverse. The kraut 88 crew let go a couple of fast shells at him also, but they exploded about 30yd from him, and he dived into a shell hole which one of our big guns had conveniently made, a split second before he got there. I told myself that he would never make it. The enemy fire, coupled with our own artillery, was the heaviest that I have ever seen in a small area. The enemy machine gunners converged their fire on the shell hole occupied by Pfc Dutko, making it, in my opinion, impossible for him to advance farther. This was not the case. After a short rest Dutko jumped from his hole and ran in a wide circle toward the 88mm gun, followed by Pvt Charles R. Kelley. By flanking the gun Dutko had succeeded in aligning the machine guns so that only one could fire at him, which it continued to do in long, murderous bursts. After running about 175yd Dutko hit the dirt and threw a hand grenade into the machine gun position, killing the two-man crew.'

Kelley now takes up the story:
'Pfc Dotko was a madman now. He jumped to his feet and walked toward the 88mm firing his BAR from the hip. He had apparently forgotten the other two machine guns; at least he was ignoring them. When he had gone about halfway to the 88mm he reached a point within 110yd of the weapon and wiped out the five-man crew with one long burst of fire. Pfc Dutko then wheeled on the second German machine gun and killed its two-man crew with his BAR. The third German machine gun opened fire on Pfc Dutko. This gun was only 20yd away and its first burst of fire wounded him, making him stagger, but like a wounded lion he charged this gun in a half run. Pfc Dutko killed both the gunner and the assistant gunner of the enemy weapon with a single burst from his BAR and staggering forward, fell across the dead German machine gunner. When I reached him he was dead.'

Pfc Dutko's heroism won him a postumous Congressional Medal of Honor.

As Company E of 30th Infantry came abreast of Ponte Rotto, an enemy machine gun opened up on their left flank from a position about 110yd away. Four men were killed almost at once and the rest took cover. Pfc Nicholas Rusinko related:
'Pfc Patrick L. Kessler, an anti-tank grenadier in my platoon, ran 50yd through a hail of machine gun fire to a point where three of us were huddled in a ditch and suggested that we form an assault team to knock out the gun, which we instantly agreed to. Using us as a base of fire, Pfc Kessler climbed out of the ditch and began to crawl toward the machine gun position. He succeeded in making his way about 50yd forward before the krauts spotted

Left: On their way!
British infantrymen pass
a significant signpost on
the road to Rome./IWM

Below: Medics rush to
give first aid to a
wounded French soldier
seconds after shellfire had
killed his comrades on the
final advance to Rome,
4 June 1944./US Army

Bottom: Fifth Army tanks
rumble over the road to
Rome./US Army

him and fired directly at him. Bullets struck so close to him that Kessler was almost obscured by the dust. Later I learned that he had been lightly wounded. Charging forward, side-stepping like a broken field runner in a football game Kessler got to within two yards of the enemy emplacement. Here he kneeled and shot both the enemy gunner and assistant gunner with his .03 [1903 Springfield] rifle. He then jumped into the gun position, overpowered one more soldier, and wounded a fourth attempting to make a getaway. No sooner had he accomplished this deed than two machine guns and a group of enemy riflemen opened fire from a position 175yd to the rear. Ten men, who had left covered positions when the first machine gun had been eliminated, were killed. Mortar artillery concentrations began to fall in the area. The picture looked black. Two men attempting to assault the machine guns were also killed. Kessler, who had been escorting his prisoner to the rear, turned him over to a nearby soldier and crawled 35yd to the side of a BAR man to secure his BAR and ammunition belt. Then, under shellfire, the concussion of which rolled him over several times, Kessler kept up his steady crawl, passing through the length of an anti-personnel minefield. The enemy, who had spotted Kessler shortly after he had left the BAR man, converged the fire of both guns on him, yet he kept going for 75yd.'

Said Pvt Alan C. Smith:
'Just as he crawled out of the minefield. Pfc Kessler occupied a position in a ditch about

50yd from the kraut strongpoint and engaged in a duel with the two machine guns. Throughout this action, the German artillery and mortar fire kept coming in. Pfc Kessler had fired about four magazines into the krauts when an artillery shell landed almost directly on top of him. For a moment we all thought that his number was up, yet, when the smoke had cleared away Pfc Kessler had risen to his feet and was walking toward the machine guns, firing his BAR from his hip as he advanced. Reaching the enemy strong-point under continuous fire directed at him, Kessler killed the gunner of each of the two machine guns and took 13 enemy prisoners.'

Pvt Richard J. Alexander takes up the story: 'But he was not quite through, Pfc Kessler had not travelled more than 25-30yd to the rear with his prisoners before he was fired on by two snipers, who had infiltrated to positions to the rear of the company and about 100yd away from him. When this happened, several prisoners made a break for it; however, Pfc Kessler fell to the ground and placed a burst of fire on either side of the prisoners. forcing them to hit the ground. Then he fired at each of the two snipers, causing them to surrender.'

This heroic deed was later recognised by the award of the Congressional Medal of Honor.

Pvt H. Mills, in his second day of combat, was the leading man of the foremost platoon of Company F, 2nd Battalion, 15th Infantry Regiment, as number one scout. They were advancing along the Fosso di Cisterna when they came under fire from enemy tanks and infantry in a well dug in position, to the north and east of Cisterna. After about 300yd Mills disappeared around a sharp bend in the fosso. A vicious burst of machine gun fire was heard, followed by a single rifle shot. 2-Lt Arthur J. Mueller, foremost man, rushed around the corner. There he saw Mills leaning against the steep bank covering an enemy soldier with his rifle. Crumpled over a machine gun lay another enemy soldier, shot between the eyes. 'I had to do it, sir, he almost got me,' said Mills apologetically. Then he turned on his heel and struck out along the ditch once more, with Lt Mueller close behind. First, Mills captured a German in the act of pulling the pin from a potato masher grenade. As the prisoner was being searched by others, Mills spotted another soldier immediately above their position and killed him as he was in the act of pulling the pin of a grenade. The advance continued with Mills still leading. Once more he rounded a bend, to engage in a duel with six enemy soldiers. He charged. 'The sheer guts displayed by Pte Mills must have unnerved the enemy for when he had reached a point

Above left: Linkup! At
Borgo Grappa at 0800
hours 25 May 1944 recce
units advancing from the
south linked up with the
forward patrols from the
beachhead forces – a
wonderful moment as this
picture shows./IWM

Left: Linkup. A corporal
from the Anzio beachhead
forces, lights the
cigarette of a sergeant of
the main Fifth Army after
the junction between their
units at Borgo Grappa in
the Pontine Marshes, 25
May 1944./US Army

Below left: Linkup. Gen
Mark Clark shakes hands
with the first GI to reach
the Borgo Grappa linkup
point on 25 May 1944. The
surrounding audience is a
good cross-section of the
various nationalities of his
remarkable Fifth Army.
/IWM

Above: Traffic control was
essential on the road to
Rome./US Army

within 10 feet of them they threw their helmets to the ground and chorused "Kamerad!" as loud as they could shout.' narrated S/Sgt Dewey A. Olsen, 'six heavily armed Germans had surrendered to one lone United States soldier.'

Enemy mortar fire began plastering the edges of the draw. Mills pointed out a shallow drainage ditch which ran from the draw to within 50yd of the house objective. It was pointed out also that although the ditch was too shallow to permit passage without being observed by the enemy, a strong diversion by fire might allow a force to proceed up the ditch while the enemy's attention centered elsewhere. So, Mills took it on himself as a one-man task force to create the diversion. He climbed from the cover of the draw under heavy enemy fire and emptied his M-1 toward the enemy, shouting defiance all the while. Then he sought cover and reloaded. A small group, meanwhile, began working its way towards the house. Said Pfc Charles L. Hynson, Jr:

'I do not know how many times Pvt Mills repeated this process but he was still standing out there firing when we reached the closest point to the house and began our assault. The enemy had been completely taken in by Pvt Mills' plan and we caught the enemy with his "pants down", taking the position and forcing him to surrender before he knew what was happening. We captured 22 enemy soldiers, three machine guns and three heavy mortars without a single casualty. Pvt Mills was directly responsible for our success.'

Pvt Mills later received the Congressional Medal of Honor.

Another heroic action was performed the same day by Sgt Sylvester Antolak, during which he lost his life. The mission of Company B, 15th Infantry, was to cut the railroad near Cisterna and capture the commanding terrain on the far side. The 1st Platoon crossed the railroad bed without encountering enemy fire and it appeared that the Germans had fled. As the leading scouts of the 2nd Platoon were about to follow, a hail of enemy machine gun, machine pistol and rifle fire burst on them from an enemy strongpoint about 200yd to the right front. The German plan was clearly to bar the advance of the 2nd Platoon, then seal off and destroy the 1st Platoon. Antolak saw the impending danger and, ordering a base of fire to be set up, called his men to follow him as he charged the German position, fully 30yd ahead of his squad. As he moved forward in short rushes across the bare, coverless terrain he became the prime target for the enemy's concentrated fire. After advancing a few dozen yards he was hit by automatic weapons fire and knocked to the ground. Jumping to his feet, he again charged on, his shoulder gashed and bleeding. Again he was hit and knocked to the ground and again he picked himself up to resume the advance. Said S/Sgt Audie L. Murphy:*

'The 200yd interval was narrowing; the Germans were firing their machine guns; their "spit" pistols, and rifles as fast as they could squeeze the triggers. They must have

* Audie L. Murphy was himself awarded the Congressional Medal of Honor for bravery near Holzwir, France on 26 January 1945 and went on to become one of America's most decorated soldiers of World War II. His exploits were made into a motion picture in which he starred as himself!

sensed that Sgt Antolak was sparking the charge and that he was the man they had to knock out.' With but 50yd to go Sgt Antolak was hit and thrown to the ground for a third time, his right arm shattered by a burst of automatic fire. He wedged his sub-machine gun into his left armpit, staggered to his feet and continued his grim charge. He advanced to within about 15yd of the enemy strongpoint and killed both the gunner and assistant gunner with a long burst of fire. The remaining 10 Germans surrendered to this man whom their bullets could not stop. Another German strongpoint 100yd to the right immediately opened fire. 'We urged Sgt Antolak to take cover in the machine gun emplacement he had just captured', said Cpl William H. Harrison, 'while we arranged to get him medical aid. He looked too weak from his wounds and loss of blood to keep going.'

Antolak refused. Again he led the attack against the new strongpoint, with the remainder of his men following at an interval of several yards. He made 60yd before being hit by the concentrated firepower. By sheer will power he managed to stagger forward another 10yd before collapsing. The squad pushed forward, assaulted the German position and overran it, taking eight prisoners. When the men returned to Sgt Antolak he was dead. 'His heroic action had enabled the squad to kill or capture 20 Germans, wipe out the last enemy pockets in the area and prevent 1st Platoon from being cut off.' stated Pfc Marion Ellis. Sgt Antolak was posthumously awarded the Congressional Medal of Honor.

Operation Wolf

Whilst the Americans were making the main breakout from Anzio through Cisterna, the British 1st and 5th Divisions were holding the left of the line, the latter being on the extreme left down to the sea, facing the élite 4th German Parachute Division. As part of the overall plan it was decided that the British troops would make a series of diversionary attacks on their sectors of the front before the main attack started, with the intention of drawing off the enemy reserves. Accordingly, the 3rd Brigade, 1st Division, made a thrust towards Pantoni on 22 May, and the Green Howards made an assault crossing of the Moletta River some two hours before the main attack on the 23rd. Although the part played by the British troops was a subsidiary one in this case, they certainly contributed their share to the success of the whole operation. As far as the Green Howards were concerned, they fought so gallantly and against such fierce opposition, both on the Moletta, and near Ardea a few days later, that their numbers were so reduced as to make their reinforcement and complete reorganisation essential. They were, therefore, withdrawn from the battle on 1 June and were unable to take part in the pursuit of the enemy whom they had helped put to flight.

This is how Operation Wolf was described in the *Divisional Weekly News*, a specially printed newsheet, of Sunday 28 May 1944: 'This attack, a stab across the Moletta River to take machine gun positions manned by paratroops was in the nature of a diversion

Right: Map 12 Crossing the Moletta River, 22-24 May 1944.

Far right: Amid a maze of wires a lineman of the Signal Corps checks circuits on Allied communications lines, whilst his jeep stands ready below. These communications were a vital part to the coordination of the Allied attack against the Germans along the roads to Rome./US Army

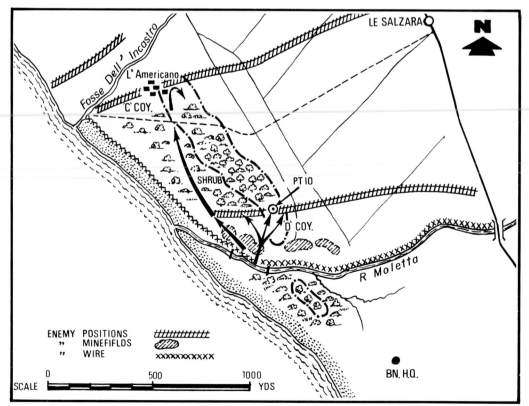

coordinated with a large scale attack in another sector. D Company of the Green Howards left at 0400 hours, on 23 May and, approaching the river, found that the gaps through the minefields had not been completed, because the sappers had suffered considerable casualties. Furthermore, only two of the six ladders by which the steep river banks were to be scaled, had been placed in position. The company collected the remaining ladders from the regimental pioneers and got away to a good start only two minutes after zero hour. The artillery had been raking enemy territory since 2.15am and a barrage on the river crossing had been successful in exploding a number of mines on the north bank and also cutting the enemy's wire. As no tapes had been laid to mark the gaps in the enemy's minefield the Green Howards attacked through it with comparatively light casualties. The advance for the first 200yd across the open ground was orderly and then, with two platoons forward and the third following closely in reserve, obeying orders not to pause regardless of casualties by mine or machine gun, they charged the last 30yd into the enemy positions with cries of "In with the Bayonet!" and "Up the Green Howards!" The paratroops fought almost to the last man and would not leave their trenches until grenaded out of them; few withdrew, and of the prisoners taken 50 per cent were wounded. At the end of the attack 17 Platoon had taken its objective, 18 Platoon had captured the central machine gun and had pressed on to try to capture the gun position on the coast. But the platoon was greatly depleted in strength when it arrived, the platoon commander was wounded in five places, and it was one and a half hours later before an attack, led personally by the officer with a tommy gun, took the post. The company mopped up various dugouts, their prisoners totalling 26, and then dug in.

'C Company, following over D's route in broad daylight lost some men on the minefield and others by machine gun fire from the enemy established to their right and rear. They crossed the river, regrouped, passed through D Company, and advanced behind a creeping barrage with 13 Platoon on the right, 14 Platoon on the left and 15 Platoon in reserve. Throughout the advance they came under fire from the enemy machine guns and, as 13 and 14 Platoons were compelled to keep in touch over a broad front 400yd wide, 15 Platoon was swung out to the left by the sea and the company made the final stages of the 1,100yd advance three platoons up. At the same time as the infantry were making a salient beside the sea the engineers were building a bridge across the Moletta under shellfire, mortar bombs and sniping. The RE officer had been wounded, but carried on

until killed, the command fell to his sergeant, and two hours after the attack, the bridge was ready. Two tanks, followed by a platoon of machine gunners, crossed the river. The tanks advanced to reinforce C Company, but the machine gunners remained with D owing to a stubborn pocket of resistance located between the two companies, which prevented them from getting right forward. The two tanks, with the troop commander throwing grenades from his turret, became mixed up with the enemy infantry and scored a direct hit with a 75mm gun on a machine gun post 10yd away. They engaged in a shoot at L'Americano, a group of houses on the south bank of the River Foce and then 14 Platoon was ordered to assault L'Americano with 13 Platoon giving covering fire. 14 Platoon attacked and became engaged in hand to hand fighting, the platoon commander, although wounded in the foot, continued to command for four hours and then asked if he might be relieved for half an hour in order to have his foot dressed. When 13 Platoon commander saw that the in-fighting rendered useless his role of a covering party, and that assistance was urgently needed, he led a "death-or-glory" bayonet charge with himself and six men. The section was wiped out (This officer had made three reconnaissances of the river crossing before the attack, two by night and one by day, cutting the wire, marking gaps, and even walking along the bed of the Moletta to ascertain its depth – each act done while a German patrol occupied the north bank a few yards away).

'L'Americano was taken and the German defenders, with the exception of six who escaped north by wading the Foce, were killed. But, owing to the machine guns on the opposite bank and the vast number of German reinforcements beginning to arrive, it was impossible to hold the houses and the remnants of the assaulting platoons withdrew to their positions in the sand dunes. Here they were reinforced by a platoon from B Company. The long salient now held parallel with the sea was under direct enemy observation from high ground to the north-east and throughout the day was heavily shelled, the concentration becoming intense at seven o'clock in the evening. At eight a tank attack was ordered in against L'Americano which the enemy had reoccupied. The tanks advanced through the dunes, pounded the houses, one tank receiving a direct hit by a 17cm shell and the other, having fired all its ammunition, withdrew before a very heavy barrage. Immediately C Company was attacked frontally by a small force and simultaneously over 200 shouting and screaming paratroops attacked from the direction of right rear. 15 Platoon kept the small force at bay for a time but what was left of 14 Platoon

was overrun by the 200 who, sweeping on, attacked Company HQ in the rear. Company HQ and elements of the other platoons managed to work their way behind the dunes until they joined up and reinforced D Company. One sergeant from 18 Platoon, commencing to withdraw with Company HQ, returned with a tommy gun, put a burst into 10 Germans surrounding seven Green Howards and managed to bring his seven comrades back with him.

'Meanwhile at D Company, 600yd away in the rear, two tanks had come at noon with rations, water and the vital ammunition, and remained at the HQ. The right hand and centre platoons of D had been taken in the original plan to attack in conjunction with the forward tanks against L'Americano and their places were taken by two platoons of another battalion. The machine gunners were still with D as pockets of resistance between the two companies had stopped all attempts to postion the machine gunners on the right flank in order to break up a counter-attack developing from that direction. Patrols had been wiped out in the attempts to capture this area and the machine gunners themselves, turning momentarily into infantrymen, had failed to dislodge one enemy gun when they charged the bushes in which it was hidden. The enemy sweeping down the dunes in overwhelming numbers overran D Company's 18 Platoon on the coast and advanced through smoke and gathering dusk toward the thin, straight line consisting of one platoon and one section of the other battalion, company headquarters and the machine gunners. By the light of a blazing tank which hurled exploding ammunition over the heads of the machine gunners, the Vickers' crews saw the enemy and weapons designed to fire at ranges up to 4,000yd fired point blank into the advancing horde. Releasing their traversing gear they swept the ground in wide arcs and mowed down the paratroopers at a range of 40yd. In fury the enemy were heard shouting from the other side of a single coil of defensive wire: "Stop firing and come out and fight!" The attack was held, smashed and driven back. Throughout the night German heavy and self-propelled guns battered the infantry positions. At dawn the expected second counter-attack did not take place, but the machine gun post on the coast, which had been cleared in the initial attack, was now reoccupied and the enemy commanded the only mine-free crossing over the Moletta.

'Shortly after 0800 hours, a message was received to withdraw across the Moletta and this, in view of the enemy's latest move, involved crossing 100yd of open space covered by Spandaus and Schmeissers. The withdrawal commenced under an artillery screen but immediately the enemy moved up

and started harassing at short range, his policy appearing to be to remain behind the bushes and fire through them. He was kept at arm's length by grenades. A depleted platoon of the other battalion formed a rearguard while the remainder of the Green Howards and the machine gunners crawled down a communication trench, made a dash across the open ground, through minefields, swam the Moletta and reached their own lines. This "local demonstration" intended to divert attention from the big attack elsewhere was not effected without considerable casualties. The casualties to the paratroops were far greater, however, and it is arbitrarily estimated that the enemy lost 200 killed, wounded or taken prisoner, in the local engagement alone. During the 30 hours' fighting one field regiment in support fired a record amount of over 20,000 rounds of HE and smoke, and, during the counter-attack, the gun barrels became so hot that buckets of water were thrown over them; later, during a brief respite, one troop actually fried two eggs on the breeches of their guns. The mortars established another record with 12,000 bombs fired. An interesting comment was made by one paratrooper captured, one of the cream of the German Army: "Your men come in

Above: Battle for Rome. Swarming up a hill with carrier support, the Mahrattas of 8th Indian Division annihilate enemy positions./*MOD New Delhi*

Right: Fifth Army troops found the bridge over the River Melfa blown so they waded across and continued their advance. /*IWM*

shouting and laughing to attack us! What can we do with men like these?'' '

Rome
'Of all the Allied units that were engaged in the final drive for Rome, the honour of being the first element to enter the Holy City fell to a unit of 88th Division. Higher headquarters policy in not announcing immediately the identity of the first troops into Rome resulted in a petty squabble among Fifth Army units and the publishing of a host of conflicting stories, most of them pure press-agent fiction. They're still arguing about it but as far as the 88th is concerned, there's no argument. The 88th was first into Rome, and the official Fifth Army operation reports published more than a month after the fall of the Italian capital confirm that claim. Apart from the purely personal satisfaction attained, the capture of Rome was important in a military, political and psychological sense. From a military standpoint, Fifth Army men had performed a feat never before accomplished in the history of the peninsula: they had taken Rome by an attack from the south. In the process they had dealt punishing blows to the German Tenth and Fourteenth Armies and had convinced the Nazi high command that they were fighting

100

men to be feared. Politically, the capture of Rome represented a lopping off of one-third of the Rome-Berlin-Tokyo Axis. Psychologically, the liberation of the Eternal City gave new hope to Italians and to subject peoples throughout the world that the sun of freedom would eventually break through the nightmare clouds of fascism. The first ray was Rome. Bivouacked in the former beachhead area after breaking through the mountains, the doughboys' half-hopes for a rest were ended with the news that the Fifth Army had all but completed mop-up operations and was ready to shoot the works for Rome, the first Axis capital to come within range of Allied forces. From Maj-Gen Geoffery Keyes, II Corps commander, came word to the 88th that it had been honoured by a new assignment in the final drive and the Corps commander was confident it would be the first to attain the objective.

'On 2 June the 88th moved back into the line with the 3rd Division on the right and the 85th on the left. The 88th attacked to the north-west with the mission of cutting Highway 6 and then turning to drive for the eastern entrance to Rome. The 349th Infantry Regiment, minus one battalion, was attached to the 3rd Division in this operation and the

Above left: Romans turn out en masse to cheer their liberators. In the midst of the jubilant throng, a US war correspondent is embraced by two happy women – no doubt he wrote a good story home!/*IWM*

Left: Thousands of Romans fill St Peter's Square to hear the Pope, following the liberation of Rome on 4 June 1944. /*IWM*

Above: Three coins in the fountain. Surrounded by Allied officers, Gen Mark Clark discusses the next move with his staff officers in Rome./*IWM*

Right: Gen Mark Clark takes the salute as men of D Company, 1st Battalion Duke of Wellington's Regiment march past to take over the task of guarding the city, 8 June 1944. /*Regt Council DWR*

remaining battalion was sent with Howze Task Force. The 351st was directed to push north-west, protect Division flanks and maintain contact with neighbouring divisions and with the 350th Infantry until that unit had advanced abreast of the 351st. In support of the 351st was the 752nd Tank Battalion. Fanning out rapidly to widen an initially narrow sector, 2nd and 3rd Battalions of the 351st cleared the towns of Carchitta and San Cesareo and at 1630 hours on the 2nd, Highway 6 was cut. After the units had reorganised, roadblocks were established on Highway 6 and parallel routes. In the assault on San Cesareo, the 1st Platoon of G Company which had been acting as advanced guard for the 2nd Battalion, ran into heavy enemy resistance. During the action, a tow-headed youngster from Virginia had a field day when he made seven bazooka rockets count for as many German vehicles and upwards of 60 Nazis. The youngster was Pfc Asa Farmer of Isom, Virginia, who was at the head of his platoon column when the fleeing Nazi vehicles were spotted. He'd never fired a bazooka before but when someone yelled "let 'em have it!" he swung into action and scored a direct hit with his first shot. Targets loomed in quick succession at the roadblock, but calmly and accurately Farmer and his bazooka paced the platoon. When it was all over a tally revealed that Farmer himself had knocked out two halftracks, a light tank, and four jeeps; the platoon as a unit bagged 24 Kraut conveyances before sundown . . . .

'In its final stages, the drive for Rome developed into pretty much of a rat race. The II Corps – including the 88th, 85th and 3rd Divisions, and the 1st Special Service Force as its major components – was moving up in the Highway 6 area. To the west, the IV Corps cleaned up what was left of the opposition and drove to Rome from that direction. In back of the line troops, jammed bumper to bumper, came all the rear echelon units from as far back as Naples. Rome was the ripest plum in Italy in the way of civilisation and fancy billets and no one wanted to be left out. For months before the May jumpoff headquarters and rear outfits had pored over street and building maps picking out the choice spots in the city for new quarters. Some far sighted brass even had selected apartment sites and villas as their main objectives in their own personal drives. Now that the city was almost in our hands, every vehicle that could roll was loaded with office supplies and equipment and headed up Highway 6. For some it was a pleasant drive through the country with a glimpse of war shattered towns to give the tour added zest. For others it was the first time they ever had been so near the front and the distant rumble of artillery or the flares from enemy planes at night inspired many a letter masterpiece to the folks back home describing how tough war could be. On that Sunday the traffic jam on Highway 6 began a couple of miles below Rome and must have extended almost clear back to Naples.

'But the doughboys still had to take the city before the sightseers could move in. And there were some nasty bits of fighting still to be done. In the 88th the final footrace got under way . . . then word came that a six man patrol from the 3rd Platoon of the 88th Reconnaissance Troop had entered Rome at 0715 hours 4 June on Highway 6. This patrol was later credited officially, by Fifth Army Headquarters as being the first Allied troop element to enter Rome. When word was flashed back to the Division CP, staff officers turned handsprings and General Sloan beamed proudly. His men had made it – and first!

'The welcome was like nothing the soldiers ever had expected or experienced. The Italians called us liberators that first night, and they meant it. For them, or so they thought, a new era was at hand, an era based on this thing called democracy and in their minds we were the people who had come to bring it to them. In the suburbs, civilians poured out of their houses to greet the first troops. They milled about the vehicles, ignored the sniper and return fire which whizzed about their heads, cheered when a German tank was hit, groaned when a Yank vehicle went out of action, cried, whistled, smiled, shouted, danced, sang, tossed flowers, poured wine and champagne and finally by their sheer exuberance succeeded in doing what the Krauts hadn't been able to do since the kickoff – temporarily stopped the Blue Devils cold in their tracks with their royal welcome. It was fantastic, it was unbelievable, but it was Rome that first night. If the civilians were glad to see the soldiers, the doughboys were just as glad to see them. They were seeing for the first time in Italy something that reminded them of and looked like home. There were splendid buildings, street lights, sidewalks, well stocked shop windows, prosperous appearing civilians, clean looking children and beautiful girls – beautiful girls in bright, gay spring dresses with lipstick and face powder and wearing shoes. And not at all bashful, Rome, and anything in it, was theirs that night without the asking. And many a doughboy got "lost" in the crowd and wound up as the honoured guest of some Roman family with food and wine and a real bed with sheets.'*

* Extracted from *The Blue Devils in Italy;* John P. Delaney.

Living in Italy

In the introduction to this book I emphasised the point that Fifth Army soldiers had to put up with appalling conditions which made even the relatively simple business of living very difficult, in the mud, the rain, the snow, the cold and discomfort of the harsh and inhospitable landscape in which they had to fight their hardest battles. In this chapter, which deals with living in Italy, I have as in my other books, tried to show this pictorially and to capture a little of the indomitable spirit of the soldiers of Fifth Army, which enabled them to overcome the difficulties and to fight and win their battles. However, I think that it would be wrong not to include any verbal descriptions of living conditions, the trouble is that they varied so often. I have chosen but one example, from the history of a very famous British Regiment – The Grenadier Guards – which tells about the battle conditions in the northern Apennines during the second winter in Italy:

' . . . and what concerned them most were the characteristics of the particular part of the particular hill which they were ordered to hold. What was the condition of the tracks – stone, mud or ice? How steep were they? How many hours to the nearest metalled road? Could you move about in daylight? Any casas (houses), however ruinous? How long a period in the line must they do at a stretch? And the enemy – were they the patrolling type, or the sit-back-and-shell type? Where were the minefields, the nearest platoons on the right and left. the closest German outpost? Of all the answers to these questions the one which the Guardsmen came to dread most was that the tracks were very muddy. They knew that this meant that they would be permanently soaked and filthy from the waist downwards and that supplies would be erratic and reliefs exhausting. To the uninformed public mud was no longer news and they reserved their sympathy for the time when photographs began to appear of soldiers sitting in snow-bound trenches. Yet frost and snow were exactly what the men most desired. Frost immediately froze the tracks into their original condition, snow filled in the potholes and until the thaw once more liquefied the surface mud, walking was not only possible but on bright, sunlit days after a fresh fall of snow highly exhilarating. Snow is far less

wetting than rain: a greatcoat and a pair of Army boots are enough to keep it off the inner clothing and it can be built up in amateur igloos as a shield against the wind. More than that, it was actually a protection against the enemy. "German shells" wrote one officer, "do not go off when they fall in soft snow. They just go whe-e-e-o-o-o-poof". And the crunching of heavy boots through the surface crackle not only gave warning of the approach of German patrols but showed by their traces exactly whence and whither they had come. So with the onset of regular frosts in December the lives of the troops began to brighten, the hills looked strange and vast, but there was a cleanliness about them, a new vigour.

Below: Pte Caulfield of Wombwell, near Barnsley, lunches on a salmon sandwich just outside his dugout in the frontline wadis of the Anzio bridgehead./IWM

'How did they spend their time? In daylight there was very little to do, very little movement was possible to keep themselves warm, there was little contact with the outside world, little fresh to discover in the familiar landscape ahead. Not more than one or two sentries from each platoon were necessary to keep watch ahead, and the remainder huddled in their trenches and blew life into small petrol fires on which they would boil themselves cups of tea. At night, especially in the early part of the night, there was much more activity. It was then that the mule trains arrived with their rations and their mail, that the patrols went out, that new minefields were laid or old ones taken up; that the Germans stepped up their artillery and machine gun fire ("It was like the jungle," wrote a Grenadier, "the animals start baying at nightfall."), and from several miles behind the front line, Allied searchlights reflected from the cloud-base, cast upon the snowfields the light of an artificial moon. Sometimes there was a family of Italian civilians to be evacuated from their farm in No Man's Land; or a German patrol dog came close enough to be shot; or a shower of propaganda leaflets fluttered down upon the trenches. So they waited day after day, in great discomfort but in no great danger, and finally, after a week, or perhaps a fortnight, the battalion would be relieved by others, and slip quietly out of their trenches, wind in long, black files down the mountain tracks to the road, and there find the lorries which took them back over the passes to the comfort of the Arno Valley.'*

* *The History of the Grenadier Guards, Vol II;* Capt N. Nicolson.

Above: Beachhead cooks prepare a treat for the boys in the Anzio wadis – quite a change from the usual bully and biscuits!/*IWM*

Left: A quick 'cuppa' after the battle. Three Tommies settle down to a cup of tea after clearing the enemy out of the notorious 'Tobacco-Factory' at Carroceto, 28 May 1944. /*IWM*

Above right: Pte Bellingham of Newcastle on Tyne, heats a mess tin of water on a midget cooker after a battle in the mountains./*IWM*

Top: It's chicken for dinner on Sunday for this group of South African gunners, of 6th SA Armoured Division, gathered round the pot in a vineyard near Florence.
/SA National Museum of Military History

Above: Christmas Day 1944 is well celebrated by these South African soldiers outside their appropriately named shack in the Apennines.
/SA National Museum of Military History

Left: An American tank crew eat a meal beside their tank after five days fighting without a rest in the Anzio bridgehead.
/US Army

105

Right: Whilst part of the crew sort out their ammo, this British tank driver plucks a 'liberated' chicken for supper!/*IWM*

Below: Amid shell shattered trees a GI gets down to some ablutions on an Italian mountainside. /*US Army*

Below right: 'A quick short back and sides please and not too much off the top!' The amateur barber was photographed in the outskirts of the port of Scauri after the Fifth Army had cleared the town of Germans./*US Army*

Bottom: A member of a 105mm howitzer crew takes time out to wash his 'aching dawgs' in the Anzio area./*US Army*

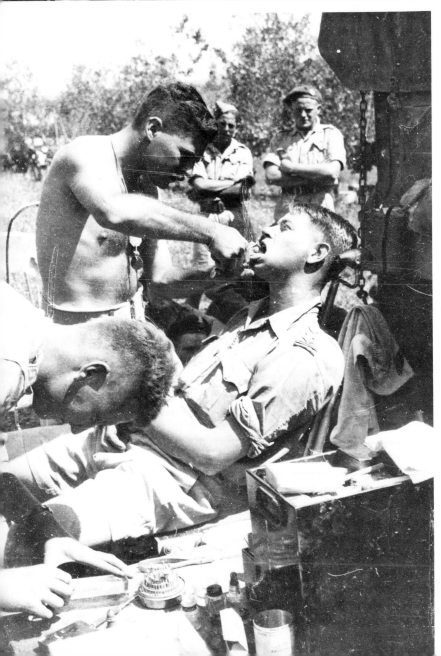

Left: LTC Hal Reese of Philadelphia, leads his soldiers in Christmas carols./*US Army*

Below left: 'Open wide please!' A South African dentist gets a firm grip on a troublesome tooth (and by the look of his muscles he shouldn't have much difficulty in yanking it out!).
/*SA National Museum of Military History*

Below: Shortly after landing in Italy, one of the first nursing sisters to land on the continent, draws water in that invaluable object – a steel helmet. The GIs used their helmets for cooking, washing, digging and many other jobs./*US Army*

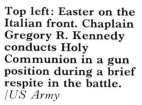

Top left: Easter on the Italian front. Chaplain Gregory R. Kennedy conducts Holy Communion in a gun position during a brief respite in the battle. /US Army

Centre left: Fifth Army GIs gather around a pot of coffee while Pfc David Madrid of Los Angeles plays his accordion. /US Army

Bottom left: GIs relax in a captured German pillbox in the Gustav Line. /US Army

Below: Mud. GIs leave their vehicles for a short rest and a smoke during a difficult journey over the muddy roads in central Italy. /US Army

Top right: 'Forward Ho!' A detachment of the Provisional Mounted Reconnaissance Troop passes through a shell-torn Italian town. Such mounted troops were organised early in the campaign and did useful work in the mountains. /US Army

Bottom right: Men of the Guards, out of the line for a short rest, form an eager queue in front of Mrs Lorna Twining of the YMCA, who had served with the unit since the attack on Cassino. /IWM

Above: 'I'd ruther dig. A movin foxhole attracks th'eye.' One of Bill Mauldin's unforgettable cartoons which so typified daily life in the Fifth Army.
/Reproduced by courtesy of Bill Mauldin

Right: This Church Army canteen did wonderful front-line service to the troops in the Anzio beachhead.
/Church Army

Below: Both sides used propaganda leaflets, these are a few of the German ones which floated down over the Allied trenches and dugouts./Adam Forty

Pursuit to the Arno

Having taken the Eternal City, Fifth Army paused briefly before pushing northwards. Unfortunately for the troops in Italy, their magnificent efforts of the past months were about to be eclipsed by the major Allied landings in Europe on the Normandy beaches, only two days after the fall of Rome. And two months later on 15 August, the US Seventh Army landed on the French Riviera. Both these operations took precedence over the Italian theatre and men and material was 'milked' unmercifully from Fifth and Eighth Armies. Fifth Army, for example, lost the 82nd US Airborne Division and the 7th British Armoured Division in late 1943, so that these two famous and well tried formations could be used in Normandy; whilst for the Seventh Army 'Anvil' landings a crucifying two-thirds of its combat strength was removed after the fall of Rome. The losses of experienced troops must be kept in mind when one examines the progress made by 15th Army Group from D-Day onwards. But there were still Germans to be fought, cities to be liberated and a campaign to be won. In the marginally better going up to Florence, the Arno River and the final major German defence line – the Gothic Line, which was even more formidable than the Gustav Line – Allied armour was able to play more of a part in the advance. This section of Italy was densely populated, with farms and compact hill towns. The hillsides were terraced, the fields interspersed with vineyards, orchards and olive groves. As they withdrew the enemy made full and cunning use of small groups of tanks and mobile infantry in a series of delaying positions on all routes. It was never easy to outflank these positions, due to the absence of suitable alternative routes and each had to be dealt with separately. In this short chapter I have chosen a typical engagement carried out by the US 1st Armored Division, the 'Old Ironsides' as they were affectionately called. They were the only American armoured division to serve with Fifth Army, although there were of course a number of armoured group HQs, tank battalions (both light and medium) and mechanised cavalry reconnaissance squadrons, together with other Allied armoured divisions from time to time. The 1st Armoured was really the father of American armour in World War II, providing cadres for all the other 15 combat armoured divisions. They also notched up a number of notable firsts namely: first armoured division to go overseas; first to engage German troops; first to land in Algeria and first to enter Rome.

A Typical Engagement

Task Force 'Howze' commander later recalled one action thus:

'One of our columns was moving on the road leading north-east from Prata. The tank company in the lead was E of the 13th Armored Regiment, with one platoon of tank destroyers (TDs) attached; also with this column was one company of the 361st Infantry, a regiment that had arrived in Italy some weeks in advance of the rest of 91 Division. It had been attached to the Division for seasoning. The column made the usual three to six miles in the preceding days. One morning, the enemy infantry by error withdrew along a dead-end road which ended in a small village. A light tank company from the

Below: Cheering Italians crowding the streets of a small Italian town as a tank of 1st US Armored Division (The Old Ironsides) passes. /US Army

1st Battalion, 13th Armored Regiment, pursued and destroyed this German unit, taking over 30 prisoners. The main part of the American column continued along the principal road, one infantry platoon working with the leading platoon of medium tanks. The column was harassed by the usual recurrent sniping, and took several prisoners who came individually out of the woods. After a couple of miles, the armoured vehicles halted in a very deep ravine while the infantry platoon sent a reconnoitring party to look around the first bend of an S-curve. The task force commander arrived at the head of the column in a jeep just as the infantry platoon leader emerged from the woods on the right of the road to report that the column was being held up by a German tank just around the bend. The doubting task force commander verified this report by climbing through the woods to a good observation point, focussing captured German field glasses on the road about 30ft below and 200yd distant. In the glasses, the enemy tank looked enormous and startlingly near. "I thought I could reach out and pat it," he remembered later. "I swung my vision left along the road and there, looking like another beached 10,000-ton cruiser, was a second Tiger. Both of these creatures had their guns levelled directly at the bend in the road where it rounded the nose (on which I was), and in the turret of each stood the tank commander, visible from the waist up, and clad in the black German tankers' uniform."

'The infantry platoon leader was ordered to gather his platoon as stealthily as possible and move them quietly into position on high ground flanking the curving road near the tanks. A bazooka gunner and the platoon leader were directed to join Colonel Howze at the observation point. When the bazooka opened fire, the whole infantry platoon was to pour all it could on the two tanks. Howze ordered the leader of the attached TD platoon to make a short reconnaissance through the high grass and brush in the creek bottom to the left of the road. After locating the first Tiger, he was to return to the road and prepare his M10, with its powerful 3in anti-tank gun, to move forward ready to fire. When he heard the infantry commence firing, his vehicle was to wait only 30 seconds, then advance around the bend and paste the leading enemy tank. The commander of the leading medium tank platoon was ordered to follow the TD around the curve, then to come alongside it, and engage whatever target he could see. The plan was simple, well understood and sound. The task force commander climbed back to the observation point and waited for the infantry to crawl into position. Minutes passed.

' "I watched the German tanks with all the happy anticipation a bird watches a cobra," he recalled; "Again and again I expected the

112

guns to come suddenly alive, swing their big noses up and blow us off the hill. The leading tank commander appeared nervous and suspicious, for he frequently raised his binoculars to his eyes and peered up into the woods on his immediate left, and once he directed his glasses almost exactly on the point where I was sitting, and we seemed to stare fixedly at one another for a long half-minute. The rest of the German crewmen were likewise upset or apprehensive . . . It was a long and trying time for us, getting ready, but finally the platoon leader announced that he was set. I took a long breath and told him to open fire.'' The bazooka gunner had used the delay to take very careful aim. His first shot was a direct hit on the front plate of the leading tank, remarkable at 200yd. The crew had just buttoned up. The

Above left: Tank repairs. Sherman *Angela-Mia* is fitted with a new engine by members of an ordnance maintenance battalion./US Army

Centre left: GIs of one of the famous Nisei (Japanese American) battalions relax in Leghorn after driving the Germans out of the port on 20 July 1944. They had a marvellous fighting record and Mark Clark tells an amusing story about visiting the 100th Battalion who had been among the first to arrive in Italy. He inquired how the recently arrived 442nd Infantry (also Nisei) were getting on – 'I'll have to check', replied Capt Young O'Kim, a Distinguished Service Cross winner and a proud veteran member of Fifth Army. Picking up the field telephone Kim demanded: 'Where are those goddam Japs that are supposed to be on our right flank?' /US Army

Bottom left: A road block caused by the unsuccessful demolition of a railroad bridge is cleared by engineers as the advance continues./US Army

Above: A Sherman rumbles through a small village on the road to Florence which the Allies liberated on 12 August 1944./IWM

Centre right: Fording a shallow river next to the demolished bridge, the big guns press on after the retreating German forces./US Army

Bottom right: Allied soldiers welcomed in Florence. Crowds of Florentines greet a South African tank crew, the children swarming all over the vehicle as Allied troops enter the southern outskirts of the city, 6 August 1944./IWM

projectile did not penetrate but did explode with a loud crash, undoubtedly causing confusion and dismay inside. The infantry platoon fired all its weapons, although only one more bazooka projectile actually hit the tank. Dust and smoke obscured the second tank but the first could be seen manoeuvring to get out of a shallow roadside ditch onto the macadam. Its big gun never blasted the hillside, and its movements were lumbering and awkward. The TD remained under cover and motionless until Col Howze scrambled down to it and forced the driver to execute his earlier orders. The command tank of Lt Carl Key went around the bend behind the TD and branched off to the left across a small bridge leading to a good firing position on the flank opposite the infantry. From there it repeatedly hit the leading Tiger tank but without penetrating its armour. Nevertheless, the Germans became panicky and tried to climb out and escape, whereupon the infantry platoon cut them down.

'A small group of buildings at a minehead occupied the small flat area from which Key's tank was firing. A galvanised-iron, hangar like warehouse with wide swinging doors ajar at each end stood between the tank and part of the road, limiting Key's field of fire. A considerable stretch of the road was visible, however, through the far door, and when the first Tiger had been abandoned, Key had his M4's gun swung to the left, and fired a few rounds through the shed and along the road in the hope of blocking off the second tank. The result was an astounding racket, a thick cloud of dust in the shed, and some blind shooting. After a few minutes, all firing ceased. No enemy tank was visible except the abandoned monster. Next morning, after more such engagements, elements of Task Force Howze discovered another abandoned Tiger which seemed to have thrown a track in mud as a result to two damaged bogies. They looked as though they had been struck by 75mm projectiles, and might have been hit by the blind firing through the warehouse; but who knows? It seemed likely that the tanks had relied for cover upon the German infantry unit which was destroyed earlier, but the tankers had certainly been negligent about outposting while they waited behind the bend.'*

* *The Battle History of the 1st Armored Division;* George F. Howe.

Below: Brazilian engineers grading a muddy road along the Arno River east of Pisa – note the demolished bridge in the background. */IWM*

Off Duty and with the Locals

Rest and Relaxation

Just as in other theatres of war, a system of rest centres was organised in Italy, in order to give as many men as possible a brief rest period in as pleasant surroundings as possible. There were of course a number of different 'grades' of rest centre that could be provided. In the rear areas centres were set up in places like Rome, Naples, Sorrento, Capri and Florence (as soon as these famous tourist centres were liberated). Here the men could forget the rigours and dangers of the front line, sleep in a bed, take a bath, visit world renowned tourist attractions and generally indulge in the pleasures and entertainments of civilisation. At the watering place of Montecatini, for example, an Army sponsored liquor warehouse was established, which grossed an average of 300,000 dollars per month, and served a double purpose by enabling GIs to purchase cheap safe liquor so that they were not tempted to buy from the back street bootleggers. Nearer the front line 48-hour rest camps were set up, many of them under canvas. The NAAFI (Navy, Army and Air Force Institutes) ran the British ones, where: 'Early morning tea was served to each man and there was no set time for reveille'. In such centres most of the entertainments were self generated, but at least the soldiers could relax away from the ever present dangers of combat. Even right up at the front special efforts were made to provide some form of relaxation. For example, enormous quan-

Below: Troops relax on the terrace of the Welfare Rest Centre in Naples. Opened in part of the Royal Palace, the magnificent view of Mount Vesuvius and the bay, was but one of the attractions of this 'Dream NAAFI'./*IWM*

tities of mail were received and distributed to the troops, especially at Christmas time – on the 15 days preceding Christmas 1944, Fifth Army post offices received 2,675 pouches and 48,383 sacks of mail for distribution. All units were also issued with turkey for both Christmas and New Year's Day. Another most welcome "relaxer" were the splendid forces newspapers such as *Yank* and *Stars & Stripes* which were widely read and much appreciated.

Even in such impossible places as 'Hell's Half-Acre' the troops found it possible to relax, as this extract from the history of the British 5th Infantry Division shows:

'There was no real "rest area" in the beach-head, but as battalions completed their tours in the worst sectors such as the "Fortress" and the "Lobster's Claw", it was endeavoured to get them to their B Echelons. Here they could at least relax although B Echelon was no haven of peace, being surrounded by such vulnerable targets as air OP landing strips and ammunition dumps. Here battalions came back to dip into the NAAFI rations of beer and spirits that had been carefully kept for them whilst they had been fighting and had some successful parties. By day, when they had cleaned themselves in the mobile baths, just down the road, they set about cleaning their clothes, weapons and equipment, checking their kit and household goods. Letters were written and read as was the gossip in the local paper from home, always of interest however old it was. In between this they ate and slept as soundly as any very tired person could and did with an eternal cacophony going on around them. On special occasions unit sports and gymkhanas were held with bottles of beer for prizes. The enemy might have been a thousand miles away for all the effect they caused even when they shelled the race track or football field or playfully splashed the hardy bathers in the sea. The mobile cinema gave many happy performances and the operator's complaint was only that his performances were often spoiled by flare bombs dropped by the enemy to penetrate the darkness. Concert parties, professional and local talent, gave many shows that were much appreciated. The pipe bands of the Division went to play to the American Divisions, to much applause; whilst American bands, also much applauded, came to entertain battalions at rest; other Americans came round with items from their stores which they offered to exchange for any non-drinkers' whisky ration.

'Enterprising amateurs built themselves miniature radio sets in match boxes and beer bottles, so they could at least listen to "Sally" from Rome, the German propaganda girl who sang with a good band and invited the Allies to come and join her for the night in Rome. Unit and formation newssheets flooded the free market with local gossip was well as their

own outlook on things of more importance. To name a few, these were: *The Beachhead News*, *The Divisional News Sheet*, *The Wadi Gazette*, *The Steelback*, *Lowdown* and others. They in their way did much towards the general maintenance of morale but unfortunately they had to be curbed before long, for fear of security among other things. The leaflet war was waged on both sides and covered all fields, both delicate and indelicate. Beetle racing became fashionable owners having their "runners" numbered, registered and even painted in their colours. A totalisator operated and serious contentions evolved around the various runners. The private "bookmakers" once clubbed together to buy a notorious winner and publicly stamp it to death, aware that the RSPCA was unlikely to have inspectors in the beachhead. There was a lot of suspected substitution and foul

Above left: 48 hours away from the line. Pte E. Clements of Littlehampton relaxes at the Fifth Army Rest Camp at San Angelo, near Cassino./*IWM*

Left: Two Springboks, belonging to the First City of Capetown Highlanders, photographed during a sightseeing tour at Pisa, with the famous 'Leaning Tower' in the background.
/*SA National Museum of Military History*

Above: Tobogganing was a new kind of diversion on Christmas morning for this group of South Africans among the snow-covered mountains of Italy.
/*SA National Museum of Military History*

Right: Cartoon page from the Army weekly paper *Yank.*/*US Army*

Above: American rodeo in Italy. A Roman chariot race in progress in Foggia, southern Italy. The chariots were made out of wheels from wrecked fighter and bomber planes and other salvaged items. All contestants were soldiers of Fifth Army or Allied fliers based in Italy and the rodeo lasted for three days 4-6 July 1944. /US Army

Left: Anzio Turf Club meeting. CQMS Sutton of Freshford, collects his winnings from the Tote. /IWM

Above centre: A motherly kiss greets this GI as he arrives in Rome with the leading troops of Fifth Army./US Army

Above right: The byline for this delightful photo was: 'The cleanup is on'. Cpl Roy J. Virden uses his helmet to wash the feet of four-year old Cleo, a little Italian girl from the Mondragone area. /US Army

Right: John de Ceasre, of Haverhill, Mass, feeds an undernourished baby found somewhere in the hills. The two sisters of the baby were killed by the explosion of a German land mine./US Army

play that would have shocked the Jockey Club of Beetle Racing had they been able to be present, but by and large a lot of innocent fun was had by all, particularly when a famous insect called "Mae West", whilst well in the lead and carrying a lot of money, as well as weight, rolled over on her back and passed out amid rude remarks from her backers.'

The Locals

The soldiers of Fifth Army, like the vast majority of Allied soldiers everywhere, showed nothing but kindness and consideration to the Italian civilian population, despite the fact that they had recently been their enemies. They were genuinely appalled by the grinding poverty of most of the peasants, which the horrors and destruction of war had made even worse. Not that the towns and cities escaped. A formal report on Naples included such phrases as:

' . . . the city was in darkness, lacking all artificial illumination, even candles; there was no electric power or gas, no sewage disposal, means of collecting refuse, or facilities to bury the dead . . . police organisation had broken down and after days of terror there was almost a state of anarchy . . . water was so scarce that each person had no more than a quart per day, and that carried by hand, for the main water distribution system had been wrecked . . . there was filth in the streets and all shops had been stripped. Food was almost unobtainable and people were starving . . . cases of typhoid fever were increasing in number and an epidemic of gigantic proportions was all too probable . . . such was the Naples left by the retreating Germans.'

119

Right: Citizens of Messina welcome three GIs with a taste of the local vino. /US Army

Below: Ferry over the Gargliano. Two GIs try to make some goats walk along the narrow ramp of this ferry across the Gargliano River, watched by an amused group of refugees who have just crossed the river./US Army

Bottom: British troops lend a hand to clean up the streets of Cava (NW of Salerno) shortly after the town was occupied by Fifth Army units./IWM

As the photos in this section show help to the locals took many forms and the Allied Military Government of Fifth Army governed some 40 million people and 67,000 square miles, which represented more than 75% of the population and 60% of the territory of the Italian Peninsula. AMG's strength was small. During the two years of its work it was assigned only 288 officers (178 American and 110 British) and 301 enlisted men (211 American and 90 British). At no time were there more than 125 officers and 190 men present for duty. Their job covered all manner of duties, from supervising finances (eg getting the banks reopened – they had been closed throughout the German occupation), to safeguarding the health of the people and preserving law and order. Indeed everything that was needed to make the area function. The American Under Secretary of War, who saw the AMG at work during his several visits of inspection, closed his final report with the following words:

'In no theatre of war was the work of military government more important than with the Fifth Army in Italy. The mission was a difficult one, with a population recently hostile and still of divided sentiments. The machinery of local government had broken down, and local resources were conspicious by their absence. Nevertheless the work was done. The field commanders were relieved of concern over civilian affairs in the rear, and could concentrate on operations at the front. Over and above that, the work had its lasting value in relief of suffering and in the building of confidence, respect, and gratitude by the Italian people toward our own people.'

Assault on the Gothic Line

Gotenstellung

The Gothic Line (Gotenstellung) was probably the best constructed of all the German defence lines in Italy. It was built by the Todt Organisation,* with some 15,000 Italian labourers being conscripted for the work. The formidable defensive positions included such items as 75mm Panther gun turrets embedded in steel and concrete bases, steel shelters, defence positions tunnelled out of the rock, wide minefields, plus an obstacle

* Founded by Dr Fritz Todt, the man who built the prewar German autobahns and the Siegfried Line.

zone 10 miles wide. The civilian population was completely cleared from the area and when completed the positions included thousands of machine gun posts, miles and miles of anti-tank ditches and barbed wire together with hundreds of anti-tank gun, mortar, and assault gun positions. About 200 miles in length, not all the construction was of the best quality and there was a certain amount of deliberate sabotage by the Italian labourers. Manned by the Tenth and Fourteenth German Armies under Field Marshal Kesselring, the Gothic Line formed the major obstacle between the advancing Allied troops and the

Below: A Sherman negotiates a mountain road in the snow. The picture shows an early production M4: note the three-piece nose casting and vision blocks on the glacis plate. With a crew of 5, a 75mm M3 main gun, two .30 and one .50 (AA) machine guns, the Sherman was the most widely used and most important of all the Allied tanks; over 40,000 tanks and associated AFVs (eg dozers, assault bridges, recovery vehicles, etc) were produced between 1942-46./US Army

Alps. The story I have chosen to describe is a minute part of the action which involved the soldiers of Fifteenth Army Group as they fought to overcome this formidable obstacle. It concerns the American breakthrough at Monte Altuzzo, which began on 10 September 1944, when II Corps launched an attack across the Sieve River towards the Gothic Line, to supplement and exploit the Eighth Army's successful breakthrough along the Adriatic coast. The US Army's official history of this battle makes the most interesting point that this, the main effort of an army of 262,000 troops (including 10 combat divisions) was actually made by less than 1,000 men – less than one third of one percent!

'The assault force that actually closed with the enemy and bore the brunt of the fighting at the critical point was sometimes as small as a single platoon and never larger at any one time than two rifle companies of some 350 men. When a prize fighter strikes a blow against his apponent, his fist alone makes contact. So it is with the main effort of a modern military force: a fraction of its bulk acts as the fist and delivers the punch in the name of the entire army.'

I make no apology, therefore, for concentrating on such a small action, for it was out of such small actions that the final breakthrough was achieved.

The Assault on the Bunkers

On Hill 926, the German had observation posts (OPs) and bunkers where reinforcements and counter-attack forces were located. A few yards south of the crest were two OPs, connected by zig-zag trenches to heavy bunkers. However, by the time that the elements of the 1st Battalion of 338th Infantry reached the hill, the western OP had been reduced to a gaping crater by heavy artillery fire. The bunkers were built of heavy timbers, with four layers of 10in logs on top, capped with soil. The right hand bunker, as seen from Company C positions, was dug in just below the crest, whilst the left hand one was some 10-15yd further down the rear slope. Both bunkers were capable of holding a least a platoon and were fitted with both radio and telephonic communications to higher HQs and to phone links in the OPs. Unknown to the Germans in these bunkers, 1st Battalion had made a silent nighttime approach to Hill 926, and were doing their best to dig into the rocky soil on the hill's southern slope. But the entrenching tools of the men of A and C Companies made little impression and most holes were less then 18in deep after much hard work, barely deep enough to give much protection. The official history goes on:

'Lt Krasman was checking the holes dug by his 3rd Platoon (Company C) when his

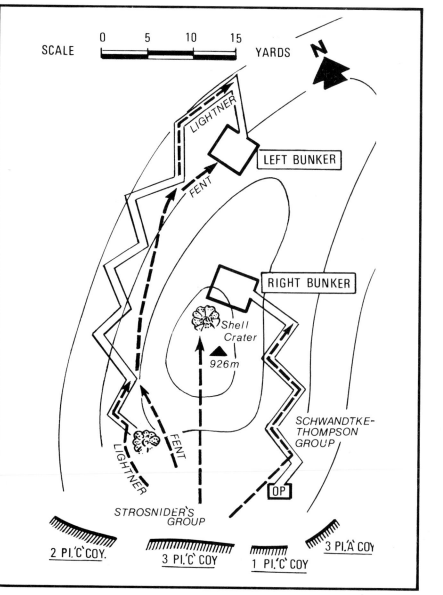

platoon sergeant, Sgt Fent, reported the discovery of a dugout which he wanted the platoon leader to see. Taking with them, Pte Schwantke, the German speaking scout, Krasman and Fent went to the nearby position, a well comouflaged observation post (the right OP). After inspecting it briefly, they started to follow a connecting zig-zag trench on the east side of Hill 926, to determine where the trench led. As they neared a bend in the trench, they spotted a German a short distance ahead. Schwantke called out for his surrender. The startled soldier darted back down the trench toward a bunker (the right bunker). Krasman and Fenton fired and the German slumped to the ground. A quick investigation of the trench revealed two 50mm mortars, a machine gun and several packs of food, convincing Krasman that more Germans must be on the northern slope of Hill 926.

Above left: Map 13 Assault on the bunkers, 17 September 1944.

Left: GIs check loads on a mule train in the Clemente area of Tuscany, before it sets out for the front lines./*US Army*

Top: Snow and frost add to the difficulties of these engineers of Fifth Army as they work to keep the roads clear./*US Army*

Above: Soldiers of the Brazilian Expeditionary Force advance with their field equipment en route for the front line./*IWM*

Above right: Machine gunners of 1st Jaipur Infantry of 8th Indian Division wearing white camouflage clothing as they man their Vickers machine gun./*MOD New Delhi*

Right: South African troops relax in the winter sunshine during a lull in the offensive. Their bivouacs are screened from the enemy by the terrain./*SA National Museum of Military History*

'Instead of conducting a search by themselves, the three men returned for help from the southern slope. After Lt Krasman called to his NCOs to hurry to the peak with some men, Sgt Strosnider and about 15 soldiers from Company C rushed quickly to the top of the mountain. Pvt Schwantke, followed by Sgt Thompson (1st Plat, Company C) and several of his men dashed to the right side of the crest of the hill and moved down the zig-zag trench. As the men neared the last bend, machine gun fire from near the entrance to the right bunker halted their movement. Several times Pvt Schwantke, tried to go past the bend, but each time a machine gun burst drove him back. Lt Krasman joined Sgt Thompson in tossing hand grenades at the enemy machine gun and at other Germans below the north end of the trench. The grenades had no visible effect. On the crest Sgt Strosnider and his group continued for a few yards before taking cover in a large shell crater. Scarcely a yard away they saw the upper edge of a dirt covered log bunker. There were doors on two sides but no firing aperture. The sound of movement in the crater evidently carried quickly to the Germans inside the bunker, for they soon cracked the door opening to the north and began to toss concussion grenades toward the crater. Some near misses jarred the handful of men in the crater, but the only grenade that landed inside was a dud. While several of the attackers, Sgt Strosnider included, remained for a few moments in the bomb crater, Pfc Elmer J. Kunze and Pfc Lawrence Markey, Jr, worked their way along the western slope when suddenly a German wearing an American helmet popped from the entrance of the right bunker. For a moment both the German and the two Americans were startled. Markey threw his rifle to his shoulder, but hesitated a moment too long before squeezing the trigger. The German tossed a grenade first. Caught off guard, Markey and Kunze darted back a short distance where they met Sgt Strosnider and asked him for hand grenades. With the squad leader's last grenade, the two men moved back on the west slope within a few yards of the right bunker. After a brief lull a German inside the bunker opened the door and again tossed grenades at the two men. Kunze promptly replied with his M1 rifle. The German drew back inside, then opened the door at intervals and threw out grenades, slamming the door each time before Kunze could fire. Sgt Harvey E. Jones and Pfc Ernest H. Becker, both of 2nd Platoon (Company C), who had been on the left slope of Hill 926 near the crest, had moved toward the entrance to the right bunker, some 10 feet from where Kunze was firing. Some of the German grenades landed within 10 feet of

Jones and slightly wounded Becker. The two men decided to try the right side of the bunker. After advancing halfway to the right zig-zag trench they hit the ground as a German machine gun from the left front of Knob 3 north of Hill 926 sprayed the area. Jones and Becker crawled to the west side of the crest and found cover in the big shell crater which had once been the enemy's western observation post. Back at the right bunker Markey paid little heed to the sound of the machine gun fire. While Kunze provided covering fire, Markey sought an opening into which he could toss a grenade. As he moved to the top of the bunker, a rifle bullet struck him in the right shoulder. About the same time, Pvt Anthony W. Houston, who was with Sgt Strosnider's small group in the crater, put a grenade on his rifle and prepared to fire. Before he discharged the grenade, a machine gun burst from Knob 3 sliced into him. After the burst the others in the shell crater spotted Schwantke below, at the corner of the trench leading to the bunker. As Pfc Kermit C. Fisher called out, "There's Schwantke, let's go and help him," he raised his head a little above the crater to climb out. A bullet from the enemy machine gun struck him in the throat and he fell back dead. The rest of the men in the crater crawled back slowly to the 3rd Platoon's positions on the southern slope and to the right zig-zag trench. On the crest of Hill 926 and along the right zig-zag trench, Sgt Strosnider's men had failed to dislodge the Germans from the right bunker. Instead of rushing the position they had waited to grenade or shoot the enemy. In the end machine gun fire from Knob 3 had forced them to retire. The men with Lt Krasman and Sgt Thompson in the right zig-zag trench, including Pte Schwantke, had been stopped short of the bunker by machine gun fire at even closer range.

'During this action, Sgt Fent (3rd Patoon), Pte Lightner, and Pte Kubina, Jr, moved to the left flank on the west slope of the peak to locate enemy positions. Joining up in the zig-zag trench west of the peak, Lightner and Fent pushed over the bush covered slope, when they discovered the left bunker. A bespectacled German officer was on top. As Lightner moved toward the lower side of the bunker near the exit to the trench, Sgt Fent climbed up and shot the German. The shot aroused the enemy in the right bunker who began to throw grenades at Fent. Dashing back across the top of the bunker, the platoon sergeant dropped again into the left zig-zag trench, followed quickly by Lightner. The two men then withdrew about halfway up the trench. They fired at the right bunker without success. Again they pushed forward in the trench toward the left bunker, Lightner returning to the entrance and Fent again climbing on top. Hearing voices inside, Fent called out in German for the men in the position to surrender. As Lightner covered the entrance – a two-part door that folded together – a German rushed out, hurling hand grenades. Lightner fired back with his carbine as the grenades sailed over. The first shot hit the German in the stomach. Slumping to the ground, he reached for his pistol, but before he could draw it Lightner shot him again in the stomach and the hand; knocking the pistol away. To make sure that the man was dead, Lightner pumped four more bullets into him. Picking up the pistol Lightner withdrew to his firing position at the corner of the trench. On top of the bunker Fent continued to call for the enemy inside to surrender and after a few minutes the Germans began to file out, one by one. Urged on by the platoon sergeant, 14 Germans, including a first sergeant, marched out. Lightner searched them, and the two men marched them back to the bomb crater that had been an enemy observation post. When interrogated, the first sergeant said that the Germans were going to counter-attack soon and would try to hold Monte Altuzzo at all costs. They had been surprised, he said, otherwise they would never have let the Americans get past the MLR [Main Line of Resistance] to the crest of the mountain. The German soldiers inside the bunker had wanted to surrender after they first heard the Americans outside. Their Lieutenant refused, and kept his men under control until he was put out of action by the American fire.

'Lightner and Fent again started back to the left bunker, leaving the 14 prisoners in the charge of other Company C men. Just before they reached the position, 10 Germans led by a medical aid man came up to surrender. They had come either from Knob 3 to the north, or from the wooded area on the north slope of Hill 926. After searching the prisoners, Lightner moved them back to the bomb crater while Fent covered the bunker. As soon as Lightner returned, both he and Fent went inside the bunker, there to discover a large store of German equipment; weapons, radios, telephones and rations. A telephone rang while they were investigating. Sgt Fent answered, but the German at the other end of the line, evidently recognising the American accent, slammed down the phone. Sure that the incident had tipped off the Germans that Americans were in the bunker, Fent and Lightner shot holes in the radios and ripped up the telephone wires, so that the enemy could not use the communications if he reoccupied the position. Fent and Lightner found fresh bread and cans of sardines, and ate greedily, for neither had tasted food since the day before. Gathering up other spoil, Lightner slipped several watches on his wrist

and stuffed his belt full of knives. The two men spent about 20 minutes in the bunker before rejoining Company C on the southern slope of Hill 926. After the second group of prisoners was brought back to the south slope of the hill, Lt Krasman, feeling that he could not spare men to take them to the rear, put the prisoners on the open slopes below the Company C foxholes. Two men were ordered to guard them from their holes. Although the German first sergeant protested, Krasman warned that his men would shoot if the prisoners tried to escape: they would have to take their chance of being shot by their own troops.

'When all the men who had been attacking the bunkers had returned, the platoon leaders made further dispositions to meet the counterattack predicted by the German sergeant. Attempting to round out the defence of the left flank, Sgt Strosnider directed Pvt Kubina, 3rd Platoon automatic rifleman, into the left zig-zag trench on the west side of the peak to cover straight down the trench, and farther to the left on the extreme flank Pfc Elmer Mostrom another automatic riflemen, to cover towards Altuzzo's western ridge. Sgt Strosnider himself, took position in the pines on the western slope of the peak. The predicted enemy counter-attack struck soon after the new dispositions had been made. Under a screen of long range machine gun fire from Knob 3 to the north, a platoon or more of Germans advanced to within 30yd of Company C's position. They tried to work around the flanks into or near the bunkers and then around the side of the left zig-zag trench. Although relying primarily on rifle and hand grenades they received direct support from 50mm mortars and machine guns. The main enemy effort came from the front and flanks, but Germans from the rear, who had been bypassed and still remained along the top of the bowl, also placed fire on the south slope of the hill. During the height of the counterattack, the 1st Squad, 3rd Platoon, Company A, was moved to Company C's left flank to fill a gap. As in other counter-attacks that followed, these men frequently had to stand or kneel to shoot, exposing themselves to fire.

'After what seemed like an eternity the men of Hill 926, aided by the harassing fire of supporting artillery, drove off the first counter-attack. With the counter-attack ended Ptes Lightner and Kubina, in search of adventure and souvenirs, headed again toward the left bunker. As they crept along the slope near the left zig-zag trench, a German from the right bunker began to throw grenades. Although Kubina replied in kind he was unable to lob his grenades into the bunker. Both men edged back to the left trench, while the German tossed two more concussion grenades. The first did not explode; the sec-

killed the four Germans. A few minutes later, Lightner saw another German approaching the bunker door, but when the German saw the American he threw his P-38 pistol to the ground, raised his hands and shouted "Kamerad!" As he stepped inside the door to surrender, Pvt Kubina's back was turned; Kubina wheeled around to see the German entering and was so startled that he shot quickly, hitting the German several times in the stomach. Kubina and Lightner helped him to a double-decker bunk and then resumed their search for spoils, taking turns at watching for the enemy. Before long their quest ended. Sgt Fent came down to the bunker and shouted into the door for them to come out.

Action on the Western Peak

'Shortly after daylight Sgt Van Horne's 1st Platoon, Company A, pushing to take the western ridge had received word from Capt King by sound-powered telephone that Company C had taken Hill 926 and that the 1st Platoon should move on and occupy the peak of the western ridge. Before Sgt Van Horne could get started, Capt King passed the word that a machine gun on the western peak was firing on the main Altuzzo ridge. He told Van Horne to knock out the gun at once. Armed with a bazooka and a sub-machine gun, Sgts Van Horne, South and Whary moved up the ridge, followed by 1st Squad. Already South had spotted the Germans, who continued to fire intermittently toward the main ridge. Moving in single file, the sergeants approached the position. They noted that the machine gun was behind rocks and logs near the crest. It was connected with dugouts and bunkers farther up the peak by a log covered tunnel camouflaged with dirt and rocks. As they neared the position, the machine gun stopped firing, but the two gunners were lying flat on the ground at the entrance to the covered tunnel and observing intently toward the main ridge. So engrossed with the troops on the main ridge were the Germans that they did not see Van Horne and his men crawling toward them about 10ft away. The three sergeants were close upon the right rear of the machine gun before the Germans spotted them. The Gunners hurriedly tried to swing the machine gun around, but before they could do so South killed them both with two bursts from his sub-machine gun. Whary set out to investigate the covered trench. Moving along the top, he saw two large shell holes, which either artillery or direct fire weapons had knocked in the trench, and dead German soldiers sprawled inside and outside. As he peered into one hole into the trench, he noticed a German lieutenant with a rifle. Standing directly above the enemy officer, Sgt Whary killed him with a burst from his sub-

Above: Grenadier Guards on their way up to forward positions – it will take them an hour to climb this ridge./*IWM*

Right: Map 14 Situation on Monte Altuzzo, 17 September 1944.

ond landed on Lightner's helmet, blowing off the camouflage net and knocking him to the ground. Kubina thought him dead and rolled him over. Lightner had only been dazed and, except for a throbbing headache, quickly recovered. Together the two men followed the trench to the left bunker, They found it unoccupied, and after a search had produced several pocket watches Kubina looked out of the entrance and saw eight Germans headed up the path towards them. The Germans were carrying machine gun parts and seemed to be moving in for another counter-attack. As Kubina continued to watch, four of the Germans disappeared from view; the other four continued straight toward the bunker entrance. Kubina grabbed a loaded Italian carbine and opened fire, while Lightner fired his own carbine. Their combined fire quickly

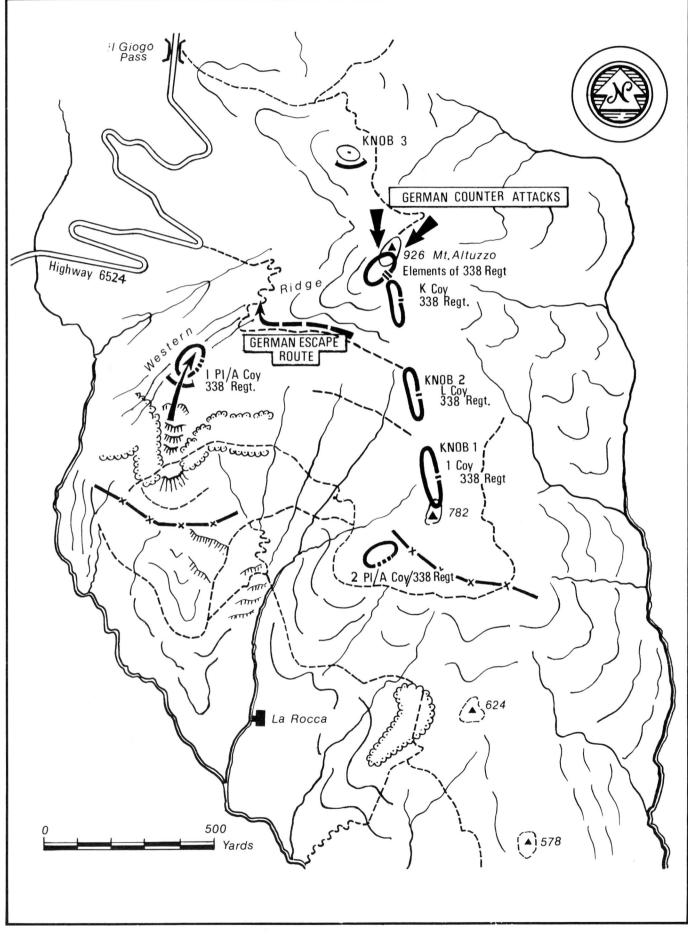

il Giogo Pass

KNOB 3

GERMAN COUNTER ATTACKS

Highway 6524

926 Mt. Altuzzo
Elements of 338 Regt
K Coy
338 Regt.

Ridge

Western

GERMAN ESCAPE ROUTE

I Pl/A Coy
338 Regt.

KNOB 2
L Coy
338 Regt.

KNOB 1
1 Coy
338 Regt.

▲ 782

2 Pl/A Coy/338 Regt

La Rocca

▲ 624

0   500
                          Yards

▲ 578

machine gun. After the remainder of Van Horne's platoon had reached the position and searched the dugouts and connecting trench, the platoon sergeant placed the men in perimeter defence. One light machine gun was placed on the peak, and the 60mm mortar just south of the peak. Before S/Sgt William H. Kohler, machine gun section leader and Pfc James F. Reid, machine gun squad leader, found suitable positions for their weapons, they heard the blast of a motorcycle which came into view moving fast toward the first house on the highway before the first switchback, Reid stood up and fired, felling the German driver with one shot from his carbine. The motorcycle bounded over the hillside. Sgt Whary, lying near the machine gunners on top of the peak, noticed movement in a pile of brush on the north side of their ridge. While he hesitated momentarily before firing, a German NCO rose from the brush, and Whary cut him down with a well-aimed burst.

'Thus, by midmorning of 17 September, 1st Platoon (Company A) had taken its objective, Altuzzo's western peak, after one minor skirmish. One German machine gun crew had been killed, its weapon put out of action, and a German machine gun crew had been captured. It was apparent from what Sgt Van Horne and his men saw that most of the enemy on the peak had already been killed by shellfire or had withdrawn to other positions. The dead who littered the hill bore testimony to the effectiveness of the supporting fire. Early in the morning, after the haze had lifted, Sgt Van Horne could see the main force of the 1st Battalion on the south slope of Hill 926. During the day, he and Lt Krasman kept abreast of each other's activities by telephone communication with their respective company command posts. The principal mission remaining for Company A's 1st Platoon and its attached mortars and machine guns was to hold the western ridge and fire on the enemy who were still to the rear of the 1st Battalion around the upper slopes of the Altuzzo bowl between the two ridges. During the day, especially in the afternoon, scattered groups of Germans tried to break out of these positions to a path leading from the western slopes of the mountain north toward the Giogo Pass. With good observation on the escape route which was completely open at one point, Van Horne's force picked off 15-20 Germans during the day. The Americans received sporadic fire from the western slope of the main ride where small groups of Germans still held out.

'About a platoon of Germans moved in at approximately 1000 hours for a second counter-attack against the men of Companies A and C on Hill 926. Although probably a little weaker than the first attack, the second was nevertheless made with vigour. The enemy relied on 50mm mortar, machine gun and rifle fire. Just before the Germans opened up, Sgt Strosnider on the left flank saw a machine gun squad of five men coming through a small space in the tall pines toward the left hand zig-zag trench. Before he could fire, the leading German, who was carrying the machine gun, moved out of his sight, but Sgt Strosnider fired his M1 at the assistant gunner, killing him instantly. His comrades dropped their weapons and ammunition and ran back in the direction from which they had come. As the counter-attack opened, other men of Company C placed effective small arms fire on the enemy. Pvt Mostrom, BAR man, shot one man who he thought was an Italian, Pvt Bury and other riflemen in positions near the pine trees on the left fired down the slopes to the west between the two ridges on Germans trying to infiltrate the left flank. Soon after Sgt Strosnider had routed the approaching German machine gun squad, enemy machine gun fire began to strike the left flank positions, clipping the bushes around the handful of Americans. Pvt Mostrom and Pvt Bruce Cohn, with BARs and Pfc John Paludi, with an M1 rifle, returned the fire. When Pvt Cohn was hit in the ankle by a .30cal bullet, Lt Brumbaugh told him to jump into a hole on top of Sgt Strosnider. Another German bullet struck Cohn's back, which still protruded above the level of the ground. The men in the right zig-zag trench, having run out of their own grenades, began to use enemy ones lying close by, and the surviving Germans soon made a hurried withdrawal. The slight respite only gave the 1st Battalion troops on Hill 926 time to feel their thirst more keenly, They had no water other then the meagre supply taken from Rocca Creek the day before and many canteens were completely dry. Up to this time the Americans on the hill had suffered about 15 casualties: the wounded were in slit trenches under the care of medical aid men. In the hope of preventing another counter-attack, Lt Krasman and Sgt Strosnider combined as reporter and observer to direct artillery fire on the area north of the mountain's crest.'

There we must leave this account of the individual doughboys' battle on Monte Altuzzo. The last German resistance had ended by the morning of 18 September, by which time 338th Infantry had killed, wounded and captured a large number of Germans, captured the mountain and breached the Gothic Line. 1st Battalion, who had battled so valiantly to reach the crest had sustained 252 casualties out of a regimental total of 290, but in view of the importance of the mountain peak to the Fifth Army breakthrough plans, their sacrifice had not been in vain.

To the Alps

Baptism of Fire for the Mountaineers

Fifth Army possessed another unique formation which, in content and training, was not unlike the 1st Special Service Force which I have dealt with earlier in this book. This was the 10th Mountain Division. The 'Mountaineers' had their beginnings in 1942, when it became clear that the US Army had to prepare itself for a variety of specialised operations under extremes of both climatic and physical conditions. This, together with the need to study specialised means of assault, such as airborne or amphibious operations, led to the opening of four new training centres in mid-1942 to teach airborne, amphibious, desert and mountain warfare respectively. By the summer of 1942 it was also clear that an offensive against the Japanese in the SW Pacific would shortly be possible, so investigations began into the need for special jungle and mountain troops. These needs led to the formation, in June 1943, of three light divisions – 89th Light Division (Truck), the

71st Light Division (Pack, Jungle) and the 10th Light Division (Pack, Alpine). The 71st and 89th had only a short existence, being reconverted to standard infantry divisions after tests had proved their inadequacies due to shortages of men and equipment. 10th Mountain, however, remained a viable organisation. The initial divisional organisation was for 14,101 all ranks (only slightly smaller than the standard infantry division), but using 6,000 horses and mules instead of motor transport. Like 1SSF, the division was initially composed of world-famous skiers, mountaineers, forest rangers and trappers, lumbermen and guides, a group of cowboys, mule skinners and horsemen, plus the regular army cadre. Their training included rock-climbing, mule-packing and forest fire-fighting as well as skiing, whilst scout and attack dog detachments and even pigeons were standard equipment! Also like 1SSF, the Weasel was much used as it was an admirable snow vehicle. They joined Fifth Army in

Below: 15 Panorama of Monte Belvedere, 19-20 February 1945.

Left: A patrol of 86th Mountain Infantry Regiment, 10th Mountain Division, load their packs into a Weasel at the start of a three day patrol into enemy territory, Spigyana, 21 January 1945. Then they grab hold of the tow rope and are off!
/US Army

Below: Walking wounded and a litter squad carry a wounded enemy corporal to the Bn Aid Station of the 1st Bn, 85th Mountain Infantry, just under the crest of Mte Belvedere which 10th Mountain Division captured, 20 February 1945.
/US Signal Corps

Bottom: This aerial tramway was built by Company D, 126th Mountain Engineers in the Farne area of the Apennines. It is just starting its four minute journey to a point 1,600ft away which would take several hours on foot. It could take 350lb and was very useful for evacuating casualties, taking four minutes instead of a hard 6-10 hour slog. /US Signal Corps

January 1945, and after various minor skirmishes, had their baptism of fire in the Belvedere offensive 19-20 February 1945, when Fifth Army finally broke out of the mountains and into the Po valley and beyond. The following is an account of part of that battle, taken from the privately published history of the 87th Mountain Infantry Regiment.

The Belvedere battle was part of the preliminary offensive that heralded the spring offensive. It was designed to keep the enemy off balance and as Gen Mark Clark explains in his book *Calculated Risk*, spearheaded the final drive for victory. The 10th Mountain and the 1st Brazilian Division were operating on the right flank of IV Corps, west of Route 64 – the ideal approach to Bologna. The 10th were perfectly suited to the winter conditions of the high Apennines, so they were given the task of clearing the high ground which dominated Route 64 from a point opposite Poretta northwards about eight miles to Vergato. They scaled a 1,500ft rocky cliff known as Serrasiccia-Campiano and seized Mte Belvedere and Mte della Torraccia in a brilliant attack which began thus:

'The night of D-Day was clear and cold with both friendly and enemy artillery sounding off at a slightly increased tempo. Company C of the 1st Battalion was already in the assembly area. Company B left Vidiciatico at 2000 hours, marching the three miles to Querciola in column of twos. Company A followed, remaining in reserve in Querciola. By this time Company F and Company G were already in their assembly areas, before Buio, where Company E was to remain in reserve. The weapon companies, D and H, had attached their machine gun platoons to the two leading companies of respective battalions, and kept

the mortars and .50cal machine guns under Battalion control. All companies crossed the line of departure on time, 2300 hours, and moved off into the cold, clear night, flashing with frequent artillery bursts. The moon was about to rise, and the long bands of blue light overhead reached sharper and sharper back to the searchlights far to the south-east across the Silla Valley.

'By midnight the 1st Battalion had moved out in some places as far as 700yd from the line of departure, while the 2nd was 300yd out. There had been no contact. Five minutes later, Company B was fired upon, 800yd out. Two burp guns opened up. Hand grenades were thrown in response, but the company was pinned down by machine gun fire and artillery bursts until after 0300 hours. T/5 Robert W. Parker of the I&R Platoon, who was to guide Company B through the mine-fields, moved back and forth between the leading scouts while the company was stopped exposing himself to the fire. Excited bazooka men were neglecting to pull firing pins and sent back the message through 1st Battalion at 0038 hours that the ammunition was no good. One of the two scout dogs, which were inadvisedly being used in the actual attack, became too excited while the company was stopped, and whined and barked. Both dogs had to be withdrawn under fire at 0030 hours. Meanwhile, Company C, at 0030 hours, was being fired upon while moving slowly through the minefields.

'They were led by Cpl Bennett L. Boggus, of the I&R Platoon and Pfc Edward D. Stackwick, Company C scout. The terrain had been patrolled previously by the I&R Platoon, and also by another pair of scout dogs and their handlers. One dog, Tarzan, handled by T/5 Clifford Mortensen, had definitely

located two gun positions on the night before. Both dogs worked successfully with the company on the night of the attack, until first contact with the enemy. At about 0045 hours, while still in the minefield, Boggus and Stackwick crawled forward, under fire from six burp guns on the company from the right flank near Corona, and cut the barbed-wire entanglements. At 0114 hours, they were cutting through the barbed wire and could hear Company G on their left. The enemy flares from Corona and Belvedere made progress slow. At about 0200 hours, the 1st and part of the 2nd Platoons, following Boggus and Stackwick, became separated from the rest of the company, and moving over a ridge, spotted four men. A flare lit up the area and two Germans could be seen running toward them. Each of the scouts nailed a Nazi before he could get close enough to reveal the American position. They then threw grenades over the ridge and moved forward. From the brush, a German sur-rendered to this advance element and told one of the men who spoke German of a dug-out with five other Germans who wanted to surrender. Stackwick made over to the bunker, jammed his gun through the port, and three men and a lieutenant came out – hands in the air. The Lieutenant requested per-mission to retrieve his helmet; and the four-some were herded to the rear. Boggus moved his group back 75yd below the crest of the ridge, from where they held off a small counter-attack from the right flank. They fired steadily at a machine pistol until the rest of the company could work up the ridge and drive the Germans back. Capt Alfred C. Edwards, the company commander, had led Company C into the attack although wounded in the hand earlier in the day while making

Above: Reinforcements belonging to 10th Mountain Division move up into the line. In the background can be seen the summit of Mte Belvedere which 10th Mountain Division captured at the opening of the spring offensive. /US Signal Corps

Above: As a barrage of Nazi mortar shells burst 100yd away, a radioman reports the position to the CP over his 'handie talkie'. Company K, 87th Mountain Infantry, 10th Mountain Division, Della Vedetta, 3 March 1945. /US Signal Corps

a reconnaissance. Near Corona, he was struck in the leg by small-arms fire and had to be evacuated from the fight. 1-Lt James H. Penrose had also been wounded and evacuated earlier.

'At 0300 hours, Corona had been reached by Company C, but B was still taking casualties from grazing fire from Mte Belvedere. Artillery fire was planned for the area between Corona and Belvedere. This was called off, for at 0320 hours, Company C was past Corona and going on up, and B was finally able to move forward. A few minutes later, B and C had gained contact beyond Corona, moving up the slope. Word came at this point that elements of the 85th, on the right, were also advancing and were only 300yd short of the summit of Belvedere. By 0430 hours, Companies B and C were on their objectives atop Belvedere. Company A was given the task of mopping up Corona, bypassed by C. They reached Corona at 0615 hours and, engaging at once in a fire-fight, overcame resistance – killing seven (counted) Germans and capturing 20 while suffering one dead and four wounded. Pvt Lee H. Chew, of Chinese descent, was shot and killed while leading forward elements of the 2nd Platoon. By dawn the 1st Battalion estimated 35 POW and 12-15 casualties. Both figures had to be revised upward. Company B, up to the following nightfall had suffered 11 wounded. Company C – three killed and 10 wounded. After daybreak, Company C, up on Belvedere, still had

a fight on its hands to secure the ridge above Valpiano. The 2nd Platoon was repelled, on its first attempt, by heavy fire and some casualties. A small patrol, from the 1st Platoon assaulted and neutralised the positions. Several prisoners emerged, hands in the air, and Sgt William F. Murphy and some others went forward to make them prisoners of war. Then the Nazis pulled their common trick – they suddenly hit the ground and other Nazis behind them began firing. Sgt Murphy of Company D was shot and killed – others were wounded. The enemy soldiers were eliminated to a man. Company D took no further prisoners of war. Company B were counter-attacked after daybreak at 0730 hours, and again at 0930 hours. They took two prisoners, one wounded and the attack was over. The 1st Battalion started to receive considerable artillery fire on Belvedere the first morning, but it was neutralised effectively by Rover Joe.* Company A stopped some sniping near Corona.

* 'Rover Joe' was a system of air-ground support, 'borrowed' from the Eighth Army, to deal with targets which needed immediate neutralisation. Forward Observation Posts – 'Rover Joes' – were established with front-line troops and manned by experienced air and ground personnel, who directed the Spitfires and P-47s onto their targets by radio. Using this system air attacks could be made well within the bomb safety line and it took only about 20 minutes on average for the air support to arrive on target.

'On the left in the 2nd Battalion area, shortly after midnight, the 1st Platoon of Company G veered right to attack enemy positions. East of their objective, the area right of Polla, they struck a minefield shortly after midnight. Ten men were wounded from the 1st and 2nd squads. The platoon continued forward, overrunning a mortar position between Polla and Corona. By this time the whole of Company G was under automatic weapons fire from Polla. Here the platoon dug in until dawn. Communication with the company had been lost at 0100 hours. At dawn they knocked out a machine gun and four snipers. They remained in dug-in positions north of the line Polla-Corona all day. On their left the 2nd and 3rd Platoons were also held up by minefields. Four of the company's partisans were killed by mines. The company was unable to secure Polla until after daybreak. Two squads reached the 2nd Platoon objective, but had to withdraw after dawn because of exposure to friendly fire. At 0330 hours, the 126th Engineers started to help the company to clear a path through the minefields before dawn. After daylight, Company G's left elements were hit by enemy reinforcements, but dispersed them and took two prisoners. It wasn't until after 1035 hours that Company G's position, 200yd west of Polla, was finally confirmed and reported to the Regiment. Company F, on G's left, had had rough going too. Their first enemy contact came at twenty minutes past midnight, and at 0200 hours, they were pinned down before Florio, while Company G floundered in the minefields. At 0324 hours, Company F was still pinned down by mortar fire, but the right platoon was flanking around on Florio from which heavy fire was coming. Florio was under friendly artillery fire by this time. It was during this flanking movement that 1-Lt John P. Benson, Jr, directing his platoon under sustained fire across a field to support the flanking unit, was shot and killed. By 0400 hours, Company F was in position for assault. At daybreak Florio and all objectives were stormed and taken. Company F killed three (counted) Germans and captured 55, losing three killed and 19 wounded. At 0615 hours the company was reorganised. Mopping up went on throughout the morning. For some time after 0400 hours 2nd Battalion was out of communication with both forward companies. The dog team of Cpl W. D. Davis and T/5 Herbert Spencer, with Rex and Mack, re-established communications with Company F.

'The 2nd Battalion, running into very stiff resistance, had to call for artillery support from the rear, and from the 86th positions up on Pizzo Campiano to the left, as well as air support, after daylight, on Valle and Marne, just behind their objectives. One diving Thunderbolt dropped its bomb squarely on one of the buildings on Polla, apparently mistaking the village for Marne about one kilometer to the north. Some Company G men occupying the building were badly battered. Prisoners came in after daybreak in batches of 12, 16 and 35 – and finally the Battalion reported 57 prisoners coming up from near Rocca Corneta. The prisoners arrived at the regimental CP just as Generals Truscott, Crittenberger and Hays* arrived to get first hand information of the attack. The impression on them was very favourable. Company E late in the morning, supported by artillery and air, took Pianello and finally captured well patrolled "Duttweiler's Escarpment" swarming all over it without casualty. Company G suffered heaviest of any company in the Regiment. By nightfall, they had seven killed and 29 wounded. Company H had one killed and one wounded.

'From the morning of the 20th until the unit was relieved seven days later, there were no major developments. Positions were steadily improved and all counter-attacks beaten off with heavy loss to the enemy. It was clear from the prisoners taken that the attack had swept over them so swiftly that they had no idea what had hit them.'

The Brazilian Division

On the right of the 'Mountaineers' the Brazilians took Mte Castello. The 25,000-strong Brazilian Expeditionary Force had started to arrive during the first weeks of August 1944. They were the only Latin American country to send an expeditionary force to fight in Europe. 1st Brazilian Infantry Division under Maj-Gen Joao Baptista Mascarenhas de Morais, joined IV US Corps, and on 15 September saw their first action, when the 6th Combat Team, which was recruited from the Sao Paulo area, seized the village of Massarosa, north of Lake Massaciuccoli. Gen Clark tells of some of the problems which the Brazilian soldiers had to face in Italy, not the least being that most of them spoke only Portuguese. For example, they had come from Brazil without proper winter clothing and their feet were generally smaller than their American counterparts, so it was difficult to get shoes and boots to fit them. However, Fifth Army rapidly produced combat jackets and winter underwear for them, so that they

---

* Lt-Gen Lucian K. Truscott, Jr, took over command of Fifth Army from Gen Mark Clark on 16 December 1944, when the latter took over 15th Army Group from Gen Sir Harold Alexander. Maj-Gen Willis D. Crittenberger was commander IV US Corps and Maj-Gen George P. Hays was the commander of 10th Mountain Division (and a Medal of Honor winner from World War I to boot).

Right: Men of the 1st Brazilian Division fire an 81mm mortar in support of their attack on a hilltop in the Sassomolare area.
/*EME Biblioteca*

Below: Men of the 1st Brazilian Division pause for a brief halt beside an M10 Tank Destroyer.
/*EME Biblioteca*

were properly prepared when they went into the line. They took part in the IV Corps major assault in April 1945, which broke through the remaining German defences and helped to spearhead Fifth Army's final drive to the Alps.

The Final Phase

'Perhaps you were there when the first Allied troops broke out of the Apennines onto the lush flatlands of the Po Valley and a delighted, but puzzled soldier asked, "what do we do for observation posts?" Perhaps you were there when hysterically happy Italians ignoring the flames cracling through their Po Valley homes and the smoke darkening the sky, tossed flowers, bread – very hard bread– eggs and bottles of wine at our fast moving columns. Perhaps you were there when the paint was still wet on the wall inscriptions that read "Thank you for liberating us. We have been waiting so long." '

The attack of the Fifth Army started at 0945 hours on 14 April, it was launched some 20 miles south-west of Bologna, west of Highway 64, in the IV Corps sector.
'For 40 minutes, Spitfires, Thunderbolts and Liberators had wheeled and dived among the hills and on the valley towns, through 200ft

columns of smoke of their own raising. "Give 'em hell", muttered the infantry. Before the planes had fired their last rockets or dropped their last oil bombs, artillerymen pulled the lanyards for the first few probing shots of a barrage from hundreds of guns that totalled 33,400 rounds by nightfall. One early round hit squarely on a mountain's conical peak. The figure of a man appeared, staggered and vanished into the smoke. One German OP knocked out. A grey haze – the smoke of our own guns – hung over our lines; puffy white clouds, then a fog of white, grey and black, over the enemy's. Nazi strongpoints in the valley disintergrated in flashes fractions of a second apart. The artillery – everthing from 75s to 240s – and the guns of tanks and TDs hit anything the planes had missed. Then the infantry, tense and silent, moved out. The crack of rifles, the rattle of machine guns, the whirr of burp guns, filled the artillery's momentary silences. The enemy was firing from the rubble of his strongpoints. The 1st Armored Division rumbled north on the left of Highway 64 toward Vergato and Mte Pero. The Brazilian Expeditionary Force moved against Montese. The 10th Mountain Division pushed forward from Castel d'Aiano across a valley studded with Teller mines, Schu mines and glass topped Topf mines that fooled the mine detectors. Resistance everywhere was deadly – with the mines worst of all. In one area, the terrain around every house was mined for a hundred yards, and every house held German riflemen. At Vergato, the mines were weighed not counted. The engineers who dug them out, under fire, reported there were many tons. The mines forced development of a new pioneering technique. A road cutoff was needed. A corporal drove his jeep across the area's green fields. Nothing blew up, so the engineers taped off that zone. Road junction 711 was not only mined, but zeroed in, and quickly earned the title "Hell's Corner". One passed there on the double – if one passed at all. Vehicles that hadn't done so littered the wayside. By dusk the 10th Mountain Division had taken four heavily-defended towns, the bare stone pyramid of 2,889ft Rocca di Roffeno and the two mile length of the Roffeno ridge. Prisoners numbered a few hundreds the first day. They were young, tough and defiant. Fighting continued through the night and the next day. By the evening of the 15th. the 1st Armored was at Vergato. A few shattered walls still stood. The Brazilians, who had cleared Montese, captured Hills 778 and 927, under heavy mortar and artillery fire; the 10th Mountain, Mte Manfino and smaller knobs.

'The night of the 15th, at 2230 hours, the rest of the Fifth Army front erupted. The sky, lit faintly by a crescent moon and more strongly by the blue fingers of huge search-lights, suddenly glowed with artillery fire-works. Again tanks, TDs and 4.2s supplemented field pieces. 75,000 rounds were fired in 30 minutes. The ground shook for miles. When the barrage ceased, the 6th South African Armoured and the American 88th Division of II Corps, pushed forward on the right of IV Corps. The South Africans advanced over minefields, captured important Mte Sole and held it against two counter-attacks; one regiment reached Capara. The 88th gained more than 500yd under deadly machine gun fire. At 0300 hours on the 16th II Corps struck another blow. The 91st Division and the 34th, veteran of three Volturno crossings, the Anzio beachhead and the drive to the Arno, rose out of their fox-holes on the right of the 88th. Their advance was slow, at first, with opposition intense. The 34th spent its 500th day of combat fighting hand-to-hand for a church near Gorgogana, about 1,000yd north-east of Mte Belmonte. It took place near nightfall. That day and the next – the 16th and 17th – the 10th Mountain fought its way into the rubble of Tole, beyond to Mte Mosca, where it repelled 10 counter-attacks, and then on to Mte Moscoso and the high ground overlooking Monte-pastore, 11 miles south-west of Bologna. The 1st Armored captured Mte Pero and Mte Radicchio, then swung north-east to conquer Mte Milano, three miles beyond Vergato, and Mte d'Aivigo, 2,000yd east of Highway 64. The South Africans took Mte Abelle despite its pillboxes and trenches. Miles of tanks, trucks, mules and marching men now choked the tight wound mountain roads, designed for ox-drawn carts. Clouds of blinding, smarting dust masked the troops in greyish dust.'*

The Springboks Start to Ring Down the Curtain

One of the greatest of the great divisions of Fifth Army from the British Commonwealth was the South African 6th Armoured Division, who won imperishable fame during their epic capture of Monte Sole in April 1945. However, I have chosen not to describe that battle here, as a number of mountain battles have already been described. I felt that instead it would provide a better balance if I were to deal with one of the Springboks final actions, the capture of the small town of Finale Nell'Emilia, which occupied a vital position on the line of withdrawal of the German forces.

The operation was part of a plan to cut off the four German divisions which were then south of the Panaro River and which were attempting to escape through a gap between the Fifth and Eighth Armies. Eighth Army

* *Finito! The Po Valley Campaign 1945;* published by 15th Army Group, May 1945.

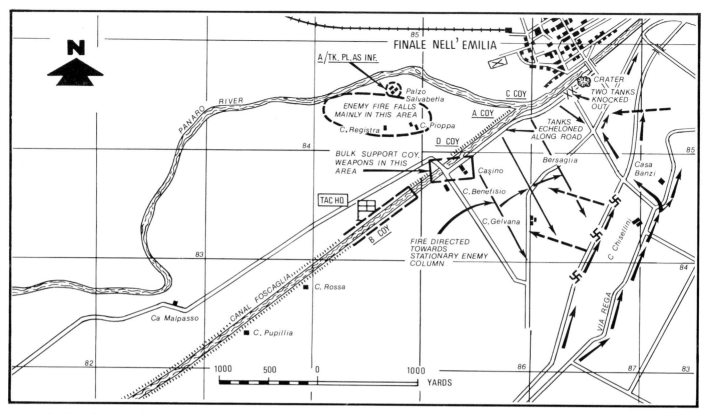

Map labels:

FINALE NELL' EMILIA

A/TK. PL. AS INF.

Palzo Salvabetla
ENEMY FIRE FALLS MAINLY IN THIS AREA
C. Registra
C. Pioppa

C COY
A COY
D COY

CRATER
TWO TANKS KNOCKED OUT
TANKS ECHELONED ALONG ROAD

BULK SUPPORT COY. WEAPONS IN THIS AREA

TAC HQ

Caşino
C. Benefisio
C. Gelvana

Bersaglia
Casa Banzi

B COY

FIRE DIRECTED TOWARDS STATIONARY ENEMY COLUMN

PANARO RIVER

CANAL FOSCAGLIA

C. Rossa
Ca Malpasso
C. Pupillia

C. Chiselini
VIA REGA

1000 500 0 1000
YARDS

troops had reached Bondero by 22 April 1945 and now the two bridges at and near Finale Nell'Emilia were the main enemy escape routes. At 1845 hours on the 22nd, Lt-Col C. Metcalfe, CO of the Royal Durban Light Infantry (RDLI), part of 12 SA Motorised Brigade, received orders to proceed with all speed, with his combat command, to seize the bridges at Finale Nell'Emilia and occupy the town. The group consisted of RDLI, B Squadron Prince Alfred's Guard (PAG), a troop of 17 pounders from the same regiment, and 1/16 Battery of 1/6 SA Field Regiment. The column was on the move by 1920 hours with 2 Troop PAG in the lead with A Company RDLI as vanguard. Next came Lt-Col Metcalfe in his jeep with his Tactical HQ, then C, D, B and S Companies in that order. The main body of tanks and guns brought up the rear, together with a bull-dozer. Here is how the regimental history of the RDLI recalls the approach march:

'Though it was obvious that many of the enemy were in the area traversed, the column concentrated on its objective. The civilian population had pulled out all the white materials they could muster, from sheets and towels, to shirts and napkins, to make it clear that they were not in the fight. Here and there they rushed out to request that Germans in their area be cleared. At 1940 hours half-tracks and other vehicles were reported away on the right. At 1945 hours the leading tanks reported that they had reached the road junction about 1,900yd from the road bridge leading over the Panaro into Finale and that

there were enemy wounded in the area. As the column reached a bridge over the canal about 1,800yd SW of the Finale bridge, an enemy column of considerable size, and of all types of vehicles, including tanks, was approaching Finale from the south by the Via Rega. It was coming through C. Ghisellini and Bersaglia, whilst another column, between it and the RDLI, was travelling through C. Gulvana. It was bright moonlight and a clash was inevitable. It soon became evident that the enemy was defending the river crossing with troops dug in on both sides of the road leading to the stone bridge over the Panaro and that the defences extended along the south-western approach as far as the houses in the Casino area. Besides these defences, an area just north of the road and south of the river, between 1,300 and 1,000yd from the Finale bridge was also defended. By 1030 hours on 22 April the engagement had become general. The enemy opened up with machine guns and bazookas from the houses and trees in the forward areas, with 20mm flak guns and tanks from the area about 600yd south of the Finale bridge and with all arms from the enemy columns on their respective roads.'

At about 2115 hours the leading troop of tanks, commanded by Lt K. P. Russell, reached a point about 300yd from the Finale bridge. They had swung sharp right over the Foscaglia Canal and then left again on the roadway running along the top of its raised bank. The troop (No 2) immediately came under sharp anti-tank and machine gun fire.

They were also held up by a huge crater in the road. RDLI debussed and deployed along the road beside the canal. A Company extended from within 400yd of the Finale bridge – at that time it was still in one piece – to about 900yd from it. C and D Companies were deployed further to the south-west and B Company in the west. It was not easy to decide exactly where the actual front line was, as the column had driven a wedge right into the heart of the enemy positions. Lt-Col Metcalfe set up his Tactical HQ between A and C Companies and then, 'sauntered along the road adjusting positions as if he were on an evening stroll'. The enemy in the houses in the Casino area, which had been bypassed, were causing trouble and had to be cleared, whilst the main body of tanks moved up and took up positions along the general line already explained.

There were innumerable incidents throughout the night, which included bombing and strafing by enemy aircraft at about 2230 hours. Some of these incidents which the RDLI history records were:
'Early in the action A Company, harassed by machine gun fire from the rear and from houses which had been by-passed, sent a platoon to clear the area. As soon as this came under heavy fire, Sgt R. A. Gibson, the platoon sergeant, offered to take a reconnaissance patrol forward. He was permitted to do so, but his patrol was soon pinned down by machine gun fire at point blank range. Instructing his section to give him covering fire, Sgt Gibson rushed the nearest enemy

Top left: Map 16 The Springboks at Finale Nell'Emilia, 22-23 April 1945.

Bottom left: Crews of these Shermans of 6th SA Armoured Division get rid of empties after a night blitz in support of the initial stages of the spring offensive.
/*SA Museum of Military History*

Above: Men of 10th Mountain Division move forward during the air preparation for the 'big push', 14 April 1945.
/*US Signal Corps*

gun and killed its crew of three with sub-machine gun fire. Leaving his section to occupy the position Sgt Gibson moved forward alone to attack the next gun position with hand grenades. He killed another two and wounded three. He now realised that he was up against the main position, so he brought up his section and led it in a bayonet charge to inflict more casualties and disperse the enemy. Even so he succeeded in rounding up 30 of them as prisoners. For this fine exploit he was awarded the Military Medal.

'At about 2300 hours a Vickers platoon which had one section under Sgt J. R. Burmeister dug in on the left side of the bridge across the canal near Casino, and another section on the right of the bridge under Sgt Norman Moffitt, heard vehicles approaching from the direction of C. Benefisio. Sgt Moffitt went forward with Peter Duncan on one side of the road and another man on the other side, to cover him. He used the only German he knew "Hande hoch!" The trucks came to a halt and, as he approached the leading truck, a German officer got out and said: "Don't shoot. We surrender." He then handed over his Beretta. Five diesel trucks piled high with ammunition and equipment, and manned by 12 Germans, were thus captured. It amused the Vickers section that this job had fallen to them. They proceeded to disarm their prisoners before marching them off when, one, who had previously surrendered, fired at and wounded Sgt Buremeister. A tommy-gun quickly disposed of the offender. Later in the night more transport approached the bridge and, as there was no mistaking its nature, the Vickers opened up. The enemy abandoned their vehicles but suffered considerable casualties. In the morning these trucks were also found to be loaded with ammuntion, rockets, bazookas and mortars. Vehicles in the rear of the column escaped, for the time being, by turning on their tracks.'

Considerable activity continued throughout the night, C Company, for example, being heavily attacked by tanks and infantry at about 0100 hours in the area about 300yd from the Finale bridge. The company repulsed this attack as did B Company who were also heavily attacked half an hour later along the road past C. Beneficio. Yet another enemy attack was made at a point about 600yd SW of the Finale bridge. This was also routed and a number of prisoners taken. The Springboks poured heavy fire into the enemy and soon the roads were blocked with wrecked trucks, the mangled remains of wagons and dead draught animals. As the night wore on there seemed to be no shifting the enemy from their firmly entrenched positons, but equally, every enemy effort to counter-attack was

138

Left: With mine detectors clearing a path in front of them, GIs of Fifth Army advance through the shell torn ruins of Monghiforo, south of Bologna./*US Army*

Centre left: Infantry and tanks of 6th SA Armoured Division push ahead along Route 64 towards Bologna, 21 April 1945. /*IWM*

Bottom left: American artillery units are greeted by cheering crowds as they enter Parma./*IWM*

Top right: A small Italian boy talks to a mixture of German and South African wounded at a dressing station. /*SA Museum of Military History*

Right: Men of HQ, 2nd Battalion, 85th Mountain Infantry make a reconnaissance of the Po River. A crossing by DUKWs and pontoon bridges is planned for that night, 23 April 1945. /*US Signal Corps*

Below: M5 light tanks belonging to 1st Armored Divison crossing the River Po on a pontoon bridge./*US Army*

Bottom: Tank Destroyers of 88th US Division roll into Vicenza during the battle to liberate the city during Fifth Army's final phase in the Italian campaign./*US Army*

thwarted. However, as dawn approached the presence of large numbers of enemy tanks and anti-tank guns, worried some of the PAG, due to the exposed nature of their forward tank positions. In fact, although Col Metcalfe gave no indication of it, he was considering pulling out of the position at about 0330 hours if the situation did not improve. A few minutes before 0330 hours, enemy fire ceased and so it was decided to hang on. As the RDLI history tells:

' . . . By a strange coincidence, light was thrown on this incident a few days later, when Lt-Col Metcalfe personally captured a German colonel on the north bank of the River Po. The captive proudly asserted that he was of the Afrika Korps and that the had been the defender of the south bank at Finale Nell'Emilia, where his battalion had been badly smashed. He decided that he could not hang on till daylight and decided to withdraw at 0330 hours. Col Metcalfe commented: "Luckily your watch was a few minutes faster than mine." '

Meanwhile 11 SA Armoured Brigade had been making all possible efforts to reach Finale Nell'Emilia, but was being held up by enemy and demolished bridges. However, by 0310 hours, the leading elements of the Imperial Light Horse/Kimberley Regiment were making contact with the most south-westerly elements of the RDLI and by 0540 Lt-Col Reeves-Moore, in command of the

Above: Two Armies meet. Men of 324th Infantry, 44th Division, US Seventh Army, rush up to greet the comrades of 10th Mountain Division, Fifth Army at the border gates in the Reissa Pass on the Austro/Italian border, 7 June 1945./*US Signal Corps*

advancing column, was liaising with Col Metcalfe. Enemy still abounded in the area eastwards of the RDLI and on the north bank of the Panaro. Capt G. E. McLoughlin, who commanded 1/16 Field Battery, has recorded how, at first light, he saw Capt L. J. P. English, adjutant of the RDLI, 'gather up the cooks and bottle-washers and advance in a spirited fashion to capture a number of Germans in a field of corn. The men advancing firing from the hip.' On arriving in the area Lt-Col Reeves-Moore decided that it was impossible to get tanks across the canal or along the road past grid 862854 (a point about 500yd from the Finale bridge, along the road leading to it from the south-west). As a result he placed the tanks under his command about 3,000yd south-west of the Finale bridge, between the road and the canal. He kept A Company in transport a little south of this and south of the canal. D Company was placed north of C, from Pupilla and north of the canal. S Company Tactical HQ and the Regiment Aid Post were established near Posse Palazzo. C Company was at Malpasso, where it took 28 Germans prisoner.

Meanwhile patrols of the RDLI had been out. Sgt C. C. Buckley, MM and Bar, ever venturesome, attempted to swim the Panaro attached to a rope. Though he was a powerful swimmer, the river at that time of the year was swift and deep, and he was carried well downstream and forced to give up. It was then informed by Italian civilians that the enemy had withdrawn, but this was, in fact, not the case. Another patrol found that positions around the Finale bridge, on the south bank,

had been abandoned by the enemy, but Tiger tanks were seen in Finale. Lt-Col Metcalfe, Maj Wilson and Capt Langton were amongst many who pushed forward to the damaged bridge in the early morning. They drew fire and Maj Wilson picked off a sniper in a tower immediately across the river.

By 0700 hours on the 23rd, another 11 Armoured Brigade column, pushing forward by a more easterly route, had reached a point about 1½ miles south of the Finale bridge. It consisted of 1st City/Cape Town Highlanders, B Company Imperial Light Horse/Kimberley Regt and tanks of the Special Service Battalion. Their arrival was a clear indication that the RDLI were about to be relieved so that they could rejoin the SA 12th Motorised Brigade who were about to strike at the Po. However, Col Metcalfe was not unnaturally very keen to complete the capture of Finale first, and went to Brigade HQ personally to try to get agreement. A direct order from the GOC put an end to his hopes and RDLI were ordered to rejoin 12 Brigade.

Although the RDLI were thus unable to finish off their mission they had achieved a tremendous amount. Large numbers of four divisions – the 1st and 4th Parachute, and the 65th and 395th Infantry – had been cut off and would subsequently be captured on the 23 and 24 April. Both the wooden bridge and the main Finale bridge had been destroyed, albeit the latter by the enemy at about 0200 hours on the 23rd, when they had realised it was no longer of any use to them. It did not impede the Allied advance as the South African sappers replaced it with a Bailey bridge in record time. In the actual fighting on the night of the 22/23 April, the RDLI column had captured 160 Germans and killed 200, for the loss of two killed and 14 wounded. 'The scene which met the eye at daybreak on 23 April was a staggering one. It has been described by Capt Eric Axelson, as a conglomeration of carts, trucks, guns, tanks, horses, oxen and mules in the indescribable disorder. In parts the enemy had attempted to get past in as many as three lines of traffic. In 600yd between the canal and the river bridge he counted the remains of 100 cars, 50 trucks, half a dozen self-propelled guns and a dozen 88mm. Coming from the Bondero direction was a similar scene of destruction. In the fields were dozens of 105mm guns, weapon pits, slit trenches, Spandaus, Schmeissers and Faustpatronen. Smouldering vehicles and dazed looking animals were still in evidence. An amazing fact is that although this terrible destruction took place up to the walls of Finale, the town was not damaged.'*

* *The Durban Light Infantry Vol II 1935 to 1960; Lt-Col A.C. Martin.*

Finito

'Two German officers in civilian clothes arrived by plane at AFHQ, Caserta, at 4pm, Saturday, 28 April. The next day, the two officers, a lieutenant-colonel representing General von Vietinghoff, and a major representing SS General Karl Wolff, signed the surrender document. All German troops remaining in Italy and those in the Austrian provinces of Vorarlberg, Tyrol, Salzburg and parts of Carinthia and Styria – 230,000 men – were to put down their arms not later than noon of 2 May.

'On 4 May General von Senger und Etterlin, commanding the XIV Panzer Corps, arrived at the 15th Army Group Command Post. Representing Colonel General von Vietinghoff, German Commander-in-Chief, South-West, General von Senger reported to General Clark for orders for the surrender of the German land forces. Dressed in his green uniform with an Iron Cross on his chest, the German commander, stiffly at attention, saluted General Clark and said: "General Clark, as the representative of the German Commander-in-Chief, South-West, I report to you as the Commander of 15th Army Group for your orders for the surrendered German Land Forces." General Clark replied: "I assume you come with complete authority to implement the unconditional surrender terms

which were signed by your representative at Allied Force Headquarters.'' General von Senger replied: "That is correct." General Clark, concluding the exchange then said: "Here are my written instructions to carry into effect the surrender conditions. General Gruenther, my Chief of Staff, will now conduct a conference for members of my staff and yours to cover the detail of the plan."

La guerra in Italia e finita!

'The Eighth and Fifth Armies had reached the end of the long long roads from El Alamein and Salerno. They had destroyed the enemy in Italy, and in doing so, had demonstrated to the world the power of coordinated action by united nations. Magnificently equipped and sustained by the untiring efforts and whole-hearted support of the "home front", the 15th Army Group – that polyglot group of many nationalities fighting as a unit for a single cause – had done its share and perhaps more in the fight for human liberty.'*

To the Soldiers of the Fifthteenth Army Group
With a full and grateful heart I hail and congratulate you in this hour of complete victory over the German enemy, and join with you in thanks to Almighty God.

Yours has been a long, hard fight – the longest in this war of any Allied troops fighting on the Continent of Europe. You men of the Fifth and Eighth Armies have brought that fight to a successful conclusion by recent brilliant offensive operations which shattered the German forces opposing you. Their surrender was the inevitable course left to them, they had nothing more to fight with in Italy.

You have demonstrated something new and remarkable in the annals of organised warfare: You have shown that a huge fighting force composed of units from many countries with diverse languages and customs, inspired, as you have always been, with a devotion to the cause of freedom, can become an effective and harmonious fighting team.

The teamwork which has carried us to victory had included in full measure the supporting arms which have worked with us throughout the campaign. The services that have supplied us have overcome unbelievable obstacles and have kept us constantly armed, equipped, and fed. The magnificent support which we have always had from the Allied air and naval forces in this theatre has written a new page in the history of cooperative combat action.

Our exultation in this moment is blended with sorrow as we pay tribute to the heroic Allied soldiers who have fallen in battle in order that this victory might be achieved. The entire world will forever honor their memory.

I am intensely proud of you all and the honor which I have had of commanding such invincible troops. My thanks go to each of you for your capable, aggressive and loyal service which has produced this great victory.

Below: The lucky ones sail home. Men of the 85th Infantry, 10th Mountain Division are pictured here aboard the *Marine Fox* in New York Harbour, 26 November 1945. Home at last! */US Signal Corps*

* Taken from *Finito* published by HQ Fifteenth Army Group in Italy, May 1945.

May 1945   MARK W. CLARK
                            General, USA, Commanding

Epilogue

'The silence was loud.

'Here, high in the Italian Alps, suddenly there no longer was the shuddering crash of artillery, the steady chatter of machine guns or the irregular blurt of rifles. There was no sound. There would never again be the sound of a shell screaming in.

'The war was over.

'You had to say that several times before it made any sense – you had to listen hard to hear nothing – you had to breathe deeply to inhale the sweet night air.

'You didn't quite believe it – the war was over and you had made it – alive. You had gambled and won where you had figured to lose. You were alive, and the war was over, and you had all the rest of your life to get used to the wonderful idea of peace.

'But you were tired, too dog-tired to celebrate, too weary to do anything or want anything but sleep. The war was over, but its end was nothing like the movies, just as its beginning and its whole bloody length had not been anything like the movies.

'You were tired; you'd come a long way for this moment; you'd come all the way – in battle – from Cassino to the Brenner Pass. And never really, during all the days and nights,

deep down where you admitted it only to yourself, had you expected to make it all the way. Now that you had, and realisation came slowly, now that the tight knot of fear in your stomach was finally beginning to loosen, you needed sleep more than anything.

'It had been a long grind and a long fight. And a lot of good men had died all along the route to help push you up and through to the end. At Cassino and Minturno, Rome and the Arno, the Gothic Line and across the Po Valley, a lot of buddies were resting easier tonight because, although their war had ended months and years before, the jobs they had died doing had finally paid off.

'Right now, in the first minutes of peace, their names and faces and deeds were hazy. You remembered them dimly. You thanked them. And you thanked Whoever you called God for bringing you through.'*

* The Blue Devils in Italy; John P. Delaney.

Below: Standing in the mud a British Tommy pays his last respects to a fallen comrade in the 56 (London) Infantry Division cemetery at Roccamonfina. /IWM

Bibliography

Aris, George; *The Fifth Division 1939 to 1945;* The Fifth Division Benevolent Fund, 1959.

Barclay, Brig C. N.; *History of the Duke of Wellington's Regiment 1919-1952;* Regt Council of the DWR, 1953.

Bishop, Col Leo V., Glasgow, Maj Frank J. and Fisher George A.; *The Fighting Forty-Fifth;* 45th Infantry Division, 1946.

Burhans, Lt-Col Robert D.; *The First Special Service Force;* Infantry Journal Press, 1947.

Carver, FM Sir Michael, ed; *The War Lords;* Weidenfield & Nicolson.

Clark, Gen Mark W.; *Calculated Risk;* Harper and Bros, New York, 1950.

Delaney, John P.; *The Blue Devils in Italy;* 88th Infantry Division Assoc Inc.

Fitzgerald, Maj D. J. L.; *History of the Irish Guards in the Second World War;* Gale & Polden, 1952.

Fisher, Ernest F.; *Cassino to the Alps;* Center of Military History, 1947.

Foster, Maj R. C. G.; *History of the Queens' Royal Regiment, Vol 8;* Gale & Polden Ltd, 1953.

Howe, George F.; *The Battle History of the 1st Armored Division;* Combat Forces Press, 1954.

MacDonald, Charles B. and Mathews, Sydney T.; *Three Battles: Arnaville, Altuzzo and Schmidt;* Office of the Chief of Military History, 1952.

Martin, Lt-Col A. C.; *The Durban Light Infantry, Vol II 1935 to 1960;* HQ Board of the Durban Light Infantry, 1969.

Nicolson, Capt Nigel; *The Grenadier Guards in the War of 1939-45 Vol 2;* Gale & Polden, 1949.

Orgill, Douglas; *The Gothic Line;* Wm Heineman Ltd, 1967.

Orpen, Neil; *Prince Alfred's Guard;* PAG, 1967.

Pond, Hugh; *Salerno;* Wm Kimber, 1961.

Prasad, Bisheshwar, D Litt; *The Campaign in Italy 1943-45;* Combined Inter-Services Historical Section, India and Pakistan, 1960.

Puttick, Lt-Gen Sir Edward; *Official History of the New Zealand 25 Battalion;* War History Branch, 1954.

Sinclair, D. W.; *Official History of the New Zealand 19 Battalion and Armoured Regiment;* War History Branch, 1960.

Starr, Chester G. ed; *Salerno to the Alps;* Infantry Journal Press, 1948.

Stevens. Lt-Col G. H.; *The 9th Gurkha Rifles Vol 2 1937-1947;* Regt Association 9th Gurkha Rifles, 1953.

Synge, Capt W. A. T.; *The Story of the Green Howards 1939-45;* Green Howards, 1952.

Taggart, Donald G., ed; *History of the Third Infantry Division in World War II;* Infantry Journal Press, 1947.

Verney, Peter; *Anzio 1944: An Unexpected Fury;* B. T. Batsford Ltd, 1978.

Wagner, Robert L. *The Texas Army;* Robert L. Wagner, 1972.

Williams, David; *The Black Cats at War;* unpublished, typed copy held in MOD Library, 1955.

Other Sources

The Story of 46 Division; privately published in Austria.

One More River, short history of *8th Indian Division;* DPR War Dept, Government of India.

Red Eagles, short history of *4th Indian Division;* DPR War Dept, Government of India.

The Tiger Triumphs; HMSO for the Government of India, 1946.

The Historical Section of the US War Department, 'American Forces in Action' series:

Salerno; August 1944.

From the Volturno to the Winter Line; December 1944.

The Winter Line; June 1945.

Anzio Beachhead; October 1947.

Finito! The Po Valley Campaign 1945; HQ 15th Army Group in Italy, 1945.